POLITICAL
SOCIALIZATION

The Little, Brown Series

in Comparative Politics

Under the Editorship of

GABRIEL A. ALMOND

JAMES S. COLEMAN

LUCIAN W. PYE

AN ANALYTIC STUDY

POLITICAL
SOCIALIZATION

Richard E. Dawson
Washington University

Kenneth Prewitt
University of Chicago

Boston
LITTLE, BROWN AND COMPANY

To

OUR GOOD FRIENDS
AND COLLEAGUES

AT WASHINGTON UNIVERSITY

LIBRARY OF CONGRESS CATALOG CARD NO. 69-12677

FOURTH PRINTING

Published simultaneously in Canada
by Little, Brown & Company (Canada) Limited

PRINTED IN THE UNITED STATES OF AMERICA

Foreword

The Little, Brown Series in Comparative Politics has three main objectives. First, it will meet the need of teachers to deal with both western and non-western countries in their introductory course offerings. Second, by following a common approach in analyzing individual political systems, it will make it possible for teachers to compare these countries systematically and cumulatively. And third, it will contribute toward re-establishing the classic relationship between comparative politics and political theory, a relationship which has been neglected in recent decades. In brief, the series seeks to be global in scope, genuinely introductory and comparative in character, and concerned with broadening and deepening our understanding of the nature and variety of political systems.

The series has two parts: the Country Studies and the Analytic Studies. The Country Studies deal with problems and processes deriving from a functional, as against a purely structural approach to the study of political systems. We are gratified that the participants, all mature scholars with original insights, were willing to organize their discussions around a common set of functional topics in the interest of furthering comparisons. At the same time, each author has been urged to adapt the common framework to the special problems of the country he is discussing and to express his own theoretical point of view.

v

182406

An introductory book, *Comparative Politics: A Developmental Approach,* written by Gabriel A. Almond and G. Bingham Powell, Jr., provides an analytical supplement to the Country Studies. It also opens our set of Analytic Studies, which will offer basic discussions of such topics as political change in the emerging nations, comparative analyses of interest groups, political socialization, political communication, political culture, and the like. We hope these books will prove to be useful and stimulating supplements to the Country Studies as well as points of departure in more advanced courses.

In *Political Socialization* Richard Dawson and Kenneth Prewitt have performed an important service for students of political behavior. They have codified and interpreted our knowledge of one of the most central and abiding themes of political theory — how men are inducted into their polities. They trace the development of our notions of this process from classic political theory to contemporary analytical and empirical work. Though research concerning these processes is in its beginnings, and the more rigorous studies are largely limited to the United States, they systematically bring in such data as are available in other countries and cultures. They draw imaginatively from the literature of comparative politics, history, anthropology, sociology, psychology, and psychiatry in their efforts to isolate and relate the many factors which affect political socialization. And in dealing with social and psychological processes as they affect political socialization, and with its consequences in turn for the workings of different kinds of political systems, they draw intelligently on contemporary political theory. They make modest claims, but their work will notably contribute to further research, and to classroom instruction.

Gabriel A. Almond
James S. Coleman
Lucian W. Pye

Preface

Although in some respects traceable to the Greeks, the study of political socialization is more clearly rooted in the social revolutions of the 18th century. It was then that the citizen-at-large became more than a shadow figure on the political stage. Not until then did social observers give much attention to what the man on the street thought or how he came to hold those thoughts. With industrialization of the economic order and democratization of the political order, however, social theorists quickly recognized that the views of the masses could make a difference. The social order depends as much on the moods and the manners of the public as on inscribed laws or elite behavior. Indeed, as rhapsodically described by Rousseau, the social order rests upon a law which is

> graven neither on marble nor on brass, but in the hearts of the citizens; a law which creates the real constitution of the state, which acquires new strength daily, which, when other laws grow obsolete or pass away, revives them or supplies their place, preserves a people in the spirit of their institutions, and imperceptibly substitutes the force of habit for that of authority. I speak of manner, customs, and above all of opinion.

It is a natural step from Rousseau's observation to a corollary issue: How does the citizen come to believe what he does about the public order? Through what processes and with what consequences are political habits "graven in the hearts of the citizens"? These are the central questions of political socialization theory. A person "matures" politically just as he matures biologically or socially. Political learning begins early in life, much earlier than is indicated by published speculative thought on this issue. The "apprentice citizen" is being shaped by political socialization long before he chronologically reaches adulthood and is given full legal status as a citizen.

Although in a general way this fact has been known for some time, systematic investigation is recent, almost too recent to merit an effort at synthesis. The earliest major attempts to investigate the political learning process were published in 1931, in the influential series edited by Charles E. Merriam, *The Making of Citizens: a Comparative Study of Methods of Civic Training*. But sustained efforts to understand "the making of citizens" were not launched until the mid-nineteen-fifties. Political researchers, stimulated by the behavioral revolution and outfitted with the tools of survey analysis, only then began systematically to relate political socialization processes to theories about political life. Within the last decade scholars have collected the information, formed the hypotheses, and suggested the theories linking political learning to explanations of the public order.

Despite this growing interest and the extensive research efforts devoted to political socialization, there has been little attempt to synthesize the findings. In this essay we attempt to draw together divergent and still inconclusive data about political socialization. It is designed to introduce the student of politics to the field of political socialization and to emphasize the close relationship between processes which "engrave laws in the hearts of citizens" and the larger social order. Although our discussion depends mainly on data gathered by other scholars, we avoid any attempt at systematic review or a propositional inventory of research findings. Our intent is both more limited and more inclusive than this. The essay should be read as a map, a map not designed to answer all questions about the terrain but to organize and integrate enough features of the landscape that the new traveler is guided as he begins his exploration.

Political socialization is a universal feature of political life, characteristic of all political societies. Though we expect to find some patterns in common from one society to the next, we also expect much variation in what is learned politically and how it is learned. Since cross-cultural variations should be strongly emphasized in an introductory essay, we have drawn, where possible, on data and examples from around the world. However, the reader is forewarned that the treatment is heavily biased in favor of a model appropriate to western democracies, particularly in the United States. The lack of comparable data from all parts of the world or from other periods in history precludes giving a systematic account of cross-cultural similarities and differences.

There are other gaps in the data as well. Some topics have been extensively investigated — how the American child acquires his political party identification, for instance. Other topics are virtually ignored — how political socialization contributes to the formation of subcultures. The conclusions we draw rest on a base constructed of fragile data; they are offered as hypotheses and speculations, not as "facts" or "social laws." It is to be expected, indeed hoped, that as information piles up in the next decade of research, all of what we have said will be expanded, much of it substantially altered, and some of it rejected.

The limitations notwithstanding, we hope our essay will provide some initial focus to a field of inquiry presently characterized by disjointed research efforts, and that it will help the student find his way about in the new and important area of political socialization.

ACKNOWLEDGMENTS

We profited from the advice and encouragement of many colleagues as we worked to formulate our ideas and commit them to print. Sidney Verba and Fred Greenstein reviewed and criticized a draft of the entire manuscript. The writings as well as the personal encouragement of Gabriel Almond and James S. Coleman aided us at various stages. Merle Kling and Norman Nie read portions of an early draft; they helped direct us to a format eventually adopted for the essay. We thank all these colleagues who made such substantial contributions to our thinking about political socialization. Ronald Gilson performed several tedious tasks in the preparation of the manuscript and also gave us the benefit of criticism from the perspective of a student. An expression of appreciation is due the editorial staff of Little, Brown and Company, whose careful editing transformed many a clumsy sentence into readable English.

Two former teachers merit special mention. Kenneth Prewitt's interest in political socialization can be traced to a graduate seminar paper prepared under the tutelage of Heinz Eulau. As his student and subsequently his colleague, Prewitt is much indebted to an intellectually productive and personally satisfying working relationship with Eulau. Richard Dawson's preparation of a review article on political socialization for *The Political Science Annual,* working with James A. Robinson, his editor and former teacher, contributed to the crystallization of his ideas on that topic.

Richard E. Dawson
Kenneth Prewitt

Table of Contents

PART I

Introduction: Political
Socialization in Political Life

CHAPTER I

The Study of Politics

FIFTY-TWO NATIONS signed the United Nations Charter in 1945. Twenty years later the community of nations had more than doubled. Within two decades, a very brief time as we usually measure history, the drive for national self-determination, coupled with forces of modernization and democratization, have brought into being dozens of new nations and destroyed colonial empires and traditional coalitions. On the African continent alone more than thirty independent states have risen out of the former colonial empires. Political changes only vaguely anticipated twenty years ago threaten man's capacity to direct his future. Change is nothing new. Man has always lived in a Heraclitian world. Twentieth-century technology, however, has accelerated change tremendously. Today political alterations must be measured in years rather than decades or centuries. Political maps, let alone textbooks, become outdated almost as they are printed.

The student of politics approaching the events of the last twenty years quickly discovers that many of his traditional theories of politics are inadequate. Especially as he departs from the familiar territory of Western Europe and North America, he finds that theories useful in analyzing stable democracies cannot explain easily the upheavals characteristic of Asian, African, and Latin American politics. To study political participation, for instance, normally has meant to study electoral behavior and the peaceful petitioning of office holders. Finding out why individuals vote as they do or how often they write letters to their legislative representatives, however, is of little use to one analyzing political participation in a country with 60 per cent illiteracy and in which violence is a time-tested way of expressing grievances to political authorities.

For the student of politics a changed and rapidly changing political world means that new questions must be asked. Raising new questions leads to new concepts and new research techniques. "Political socialization" is one of these new concepts. It directs attention to a political problem only dimly appreciated in most pre-World War II political analysis.

Political socialization has to do with "people oriented" explanations of political events. It is a concept directing attention toward the knowledge, values, and beliefs of the average citizen. What is it that the citizen wants of his government? Is he willing to support the political rules and rulers? Under what conditions? Political socialization theory assumes that citizens in different nations come to feel and believe differently about their political leaders and structures. For instance, the average German seems to know a great deal about his government officials and their policies. The average Brazilian peasant, on the other hand, knows little about events in Brasilia. Britons, on the whole, appear to trust their fellow citizens and to respect their political leaders. Widespread social and political mistrust seem to permeate the Italian political culture. Inspired by a frontier ideology, Americans approach political life with a sense of their power to shape and mold political events. The South African Bantu, in contrast, tends to look upon political events as he does the weather, with fatalistic resignation.

Political socialization theory also assumes that the various attitudes citizens have toward political life affect the way in which the state operates. It raises the question of how the qualities of a people relate to political forms and practices. What social cement has held the United States together as one nation despite a brother-against-brother civil war? What values of the German people permitted Hitler's rise to power and his pathological exercise of that power? What characteristics of the Nigerian people prevent a stable national government from being established in their country? What is it about the British which gives such continuity and stability to their political life?

These questions share a basic assumption. A nation's political life is linked closely to the moods, manners, and values of its people. What citizens believe and feel about politics both reflect and shape the politics of their nation. On the one hand a continually ineffective government will lose the confidence of its population. On the other, a widespread lack of confidence in a government is likely to render the government ineffective. These are, of course, not completely new notions in political studies. A very perceptive nineteenth-century French visitor to the United States, Alexis de Tocqueville, analyzed the social foundations of democratic processes in America, emphasizing just these relationships. His explanation is as instructive today as it was 130 years ago. Tocqueville singled out the special attitudes and values of the American people. The country's physical conditions and legal structures were important, he allowed, but the manners and customs of the inhabitants were of the greatest import:

> These three great causes serve, no doubt, to regulate and direct American democracy; but if they were to be classed in their proper order, I should say that physical circumstances are less efficient than the laws, and the laws less so than the customs of the people. I am convinced that the most advantageous situation and the best possible laws cannot maintain a constitution in spite of the customs of a country; while the latter may turn to some advantage the most unfavorable positions and the worst laws. The importance of customs is a common truth to which study and experience incessantly direct our attention.[1]

The "common truth" that political customs "regulate and direct" political life is an assumption political socialization theory shares with Tocqueville. Working with this assumption, students of politics are asking about the sources of political customs and values: What social mechanisms provide a nation with its peculiar political customs? Part of the answer to this question, as we attempt to make clear in this essay,

[1] Alexis de Tocqueville, *Democracy in America* (New York: Knopf, 1960), I, p. 322.

is found in political socialization. "Political socialization" is the name given the processes through which a citizen acquires his own view of the political world. The school child pledging allegiance to the flag each morning or learning from experiences with teachers that authorities command obedience is being politically socialized. Social experiences of a wide variety become relevant for the ways in which the child, the adolescent, and the adult will view political matters. Viewed from another perspective, political socialization is the way in which one generation passes on political standards and beliefs to succeeding generations. "Cultural transmission" is the phrase that best describes this process. Through both deliberate official political education programs and the passing on of political norms in less deliberate and more informal groups such as the family and peer groups, societies ensure intergenerational continuity in political attitudes and values. These efforts and processes are the crux of political socialization and are the major subject of this essay.

HISTORICAL AND INTELLECTUAL ROOTS
OF POLITICAL SOCIALIZATION

Like other concepts recently added to the vocabulary of political science, the expression "socialization" predates its direct application to political study. We can identify three broad topics which help us understand the roots of the concept: (1) the classical literature of political theory; (2) intellectual issues in other behavioral sciences; and (3) contemporary political events. In briefly tracing how the term "political socialization" has come into use we will be aided by understanding the various problems with which it deals in each of these areas.

1. *The Classical Literature of Political Theory.* Though the phrase "political socialization" is of recent vintage, the ways of preparing individuals for citizenship and the consequences of such preparation for the state have long been of interest to political theorists. In *The Republic,* Plato devoted much attention to education and childhood experiences as the arena and means for instilling appropriate citizenship values. He outlined a complex training procedure designed to ensure

that the various classes of citizens would be fitted with values and predispositions appropriate to their differentiated participant roles in the *Polis*. Plato argued that citizens' values affect the stability and order of political institutions. He attributed the cyclical degeneration of politics to defects in political education; to failures in political socialization.

Aristotle likewise emphasized political education. He stressed the relationship between character types and constitutional structures. Different political structures require different types of political values and predispositions. Aspects of political education, political character, and their relationships to behavior and institutions have been of at least peripheral interest to most political theorists. We have mentioned already the importance Tocqueville placed upon political manners in his analysis of the persisting democratic institutions in early nineteenth-century America.

The study of political training, on the one hand, is not a departure from intellectual themes raised by centuries of social theorists. How people acquire their political views and how political regimes maintain themselves by ensuring appropriate political outlooks are issues which continue a long tradition of scholarly inquiry. On the other hand, the self-conscious attention to the political masses and their views is a departure. As we shall make clearer presently, democratic ideology and mass participation in politics represent a sharp break in political practices. Contemporary focus on political socialization represents an interruption in scholarly inquiry that reflects changes in the political world. The rigor, systemization, and method through which "citizenship training" questions are posed and studied are also a contemporary development.

2. *Roots in Other Behavioral Sciences*. Students of political socialization also have drawn upon other behavioral sciences, especially social anthropology, psychiatry, social psychology, and sociology. Each of these disciplines inquires into socialization — the process by which children, born with an enormous potential for different types of behavior, come to adopt the specific standards of their own society.

Socialization hypotheses and supportive evidence of cultural anthropologists are especially relevant to the contemporary attention to political socialization. Anthropologists, studying diverse cultures, discovered early that social behavior varied greatly from society to society. One society might be dominated by aggressive, achievement oriented males, whereas in another society males were generally passive. Polygamy was practiced in one culture and frowned upon in another. The anthropological observation stressing cultural relativism has been coupled with a second realization. Within a society behavior patterns exhibit considerable persistence and stability over time. Tradition has been a major guide to behavior, and ancestors are models for behavior.

As the cultural anthropologist looked closely at uniformities within cultures and differences between cultures he was impressed with the way in which cultural values are transmitted from one generation to another. The many forms of social learning indigenous to a society seemed to ensure that each generation more or less replicated the behavior of the parent generation. Children, at a very early age, begin to pick up cues from parents and peers about how to behave in various situations. Fighting with siblings is either culturally approved or is not. Children are "socialized" into the norms appropriate for their own society. Anthropologists labeled the process of social learning or cultural transmission "socialization." [2]

Early anthropologists primarily investigated non-Western and traditional cultures. Nazism and World War II presented new issues and a new arena for students of cultural development and transmission. Investigations of "national character" or "modal personality" became popular as researchers sought to describe and explain the behavior of the warring nations. In particular, there were numerous attempts to explain the rise of fascism and the German war movement. Psychoanalyst Erich Fromm's analysis of the relationship between the au-

---

[2] See, for example, Ruth Benedict, *Patterns of Culture* (Boston: Houghton Mifflin, 1934); Ralph Linton, *The Cultural Background of Personality* (New York: Appleton-Century-Crofts, 1945); Margaret Mead, *Coming of Age in Samoa* (New York: Morrow, 1928); and her *From the South Seas* (New York: Morrow, 1939).

thoritarianism of German Lutheranism and German fascism was one of the more influential treatises of this kind. Another example is Geoffrey Gorer's analysis of Russian character as influenced by childhood swaddling. He suggested that this childhood experience led to passivity and controlled rage in adulthood, an important aspect of Russian character.[3]

The work of cultural anthropologists on socialization has been relevant to contemporary interest in political socialization for several reasons. The specific anthropological findings about socialization, cultural transmission, and personality development are often applicable to more specific political socialization. The anthropologists have collected data about primitive and non-Western societies which are of use as political observers shift attention to the non-Western world. Anthropologists also helped improve techniques and methods of research directly applicable to crosscultural political analysis.

The field of psychiatry is another source of hypotheses about socialization. The various psychoanalytic schools with their emphasis on personality development are particularly rich in ideas. Reflecting Freudian roots, much psychoanalytic theory stresses how early childhood experiences influence adult social values. Whereas the anthropologists sensitized political scientists to socialization as transmission of cultural values, psychiatry has contributed hypotheses about socialization processes and personality development.[4] The two most important notions that psychoanalytic theory has contributed to an understanding of political socialization are the con-

[3] Erich Fromm, *Escape from Freedom* (New York: Holt, 1941); and G. Gorer and J. Rickman, *The People of Great Russia* (London: Crosset Press, 1949).

[4] See Sigmund Freud, *The Basic Writings of Sigmund Freud* (New York: Random House, 1938) for the work of Freud himself. For a general discussion of the psychoanalytic approach see G. S. Blum, *Psychoanalytic Theory of Personality* (New York: McGraw-Hill, 1953). For works that combine psychological and anthropological notions, see A. Davis and J. Dollard, *Children of Bondage* (Washington, D.C.: American Council on Education, 1940); A. Kardiner and Ralph Linton, *The Individual and His Society* (New York: Columbia University Press, 1939); *The Psychological Frontiers of Society* (New York: Columbia University Press, 1945); and John W. M. Whiting and Irvin L. Child, *Child Training and Personality* (New Haven: Yale University Press, 1953).

ceptualization of personality and attitudes as structured developmental phenomena and attention to the significance of early childhood experiences in the formation of political attitudes and values.

A third body of scholarly work nurturing the study of political socialization is found in sociology and social psychology. Here the emphasis has been on how group standards are passed on to individual members. Sociologists, at least as far back as Cooley at the beginning of the twentieth century, emphasized how group relationships affect attitudes and behavior, and how members' orientations affect group life. At present there are a great many propositions dealing with how groups pass on norms and train their members for positions in society.[5] These sociological notions of group influence have been used by political scientists studying political attitude formation and political behavior.

A corollary area of sociological theory relevant for understanding political socialization is social role analysis. In a line of inquiry stemming from the work of Cooley and Mead, social theorists have observed that assuming a role — that of a citizen, for example — is to take on behavior expected of persons in that role.[6] One learns how to be a father, in part, by discovering what society expects of fathers. For George Herbert Mead the socialization process involves discovering what it is that society expects of us in our various roles. The child discovers "himself" as he discovers what society is. He forms a "social self" in response to the expectations directed toward him from parents, peers, teachers, and other "significant others." If mother expects him to be clean, obedient, and prompt, cleanliness, obedience, and promptness become part of his self. As the child matures he discovers that society in general — what Mead called the "generalized other" — is little

[5] For collections and summaries of literature on groups, see D. Cartwright and A. Zander, *Group Dynamics* (New York: Harper & Row, 1962); A. P. Hare, *et al.* (eds.), *Small Groups: Studies in Social Interaction* (New York: Knopf, 1955); and Sidney Verba, *Small Groups and Political Behavior* (Princeton: Princeton University Press, 1961).

[6] See Charles H. Cooley, *Human Nature and the Social Order* (Boston: Scribner, 1902); and George Herbert Mead, *Mind, Self and Society* (Chicago: University of Chicago Press, 1934).

more than a package of expectations about how he, the child, should behave. The socialized child is one who has discovered and behaves in a manner consistent with society's expectations.

Sometimes implicitly and sometimes explicitly, students of politics have borrowed from and built upon the cultural-anthropological, the culture-personality, the group-dynamics, and the social-role interpretations of socialization. As we shall see a bit later the notions of cultural transmission and social role are especially relevant to understanding political socialization.

3. *Recent Developments in the Study of Politics*. What is happening in the "real" political world, as we might expect, conditions the concepts with which political scientists work. We have remarked that a rapidly changing political world has brought about a rapidly changing political science. We shall cite just one example. The past two centuries witnessed a "participation explosion" in politics. Beginning in Great Britain and the United States, then moving to other Western European countries, and now spread around the globe, the democratic ideology with its emphasis on citizen participation has permeated political life, in form and discourse if not always in practice. Professional students of politics have not been indifferent to the consequences an expanding franchise and political participation have brought.

Beginning in the 1920's, students of politics began to investigate voting behavior, party identification, and political ideology, attitudes, and opinions.[7] Interest in these areas was greatly accelerated by the development of techniques of survey sampling, interviewing, questionnaire design, and opinion and personality measurement during the 1930's and 1940's. By the late 1950's, social scientists in the United States and Europe had accumulated a great deal of information on how voting behavior and political attitudes were related to under-

---

[7] For some of the earliest of these efforts, see S. A. Rice, *Quantitative Methods in Politics* (New York: Knopf, 1928); H. Tingsten, *Political Behavior: Studies in Election Statistics,* Stockholm Economic Studies, No. 7 (London: P. S. King, 1937); and Charles E. Merriam and Harold F. Gosnell, *Non-Voting: Causes and Methods of Control* (Chicago: University of Chicago Press, 1924).

lying economic, sociological, and psychological conditions.[8] As this knowledge accumulated, political scientists became interested in how people came to hold specific party identifications, maintain certain political values, and take stands on issues. The role of the family, school, and group experiences in forming these political orientations became an important subject of investigation. In the early 1950's, the name "political socialization" was introduced to refer to this process of political learning.

The first systematic review of the findings appeared in Herbert Hyman's *Political Socialization* (1959).[9] In 1960, Fred Greenstein and David Easton with Robert Hess reported almost simultaneously on the results of their respective research on the development of political orientations in school children.[10] At about the same time Heinz Eulau and his associates were using the conceptual apparatus of political socialization to study the recruitment and careers of political office holders.[11]

Concurrently with this focus on how individuals acquire their political orientations, the expression "political socialization" came into use in research and theory focusing on political systems and political development. Socialization as a political system function was used by Almond, Coleman, and others in *The Politics of the Developing Areas* (1960), by Lucian Pye in "Political Modernization and Research on the Process of Political Socialization" (1959), and was discussed by David Easton and Robert Hess in a paper entitled, "Some Problems

[8] For examples, inventories, and analysis of this research see B. Berelson, P. F. Lazarsfeld, and W. N. McPhee, *Voting* (Chicago: University of Chicago Press, 1954); Eugene Burdick and Arthur J. Brodbeck, *American Voting Behavior* (New York: The Free Press, 1959); and Robert E. Lane, *Political Life: Why People Get Involved in Politics* (New York: The Free Press, 1959).

[9] Herbert H. Hyman, *Political Socialization* (New York: The Free Press, 1959).

[10] Robert D. Hess and David Easton, "The Child's Changing Image of the President," *The Public Opinion Quarterly*, XXIV (1960), pp. 632–644; and Fred I. Greenstein, "The Benevolent Leader: Children's Images of Political Authority," *American Political Science Review*, LIV (1960), pp. 934–943.

[11] Heinz Eulau, *et al.*, "Socialization of American State Legislators," *Midwest Journal of Political Science*, III (1959), pp. 188–206.

in the Study of Political Socialization" (1958).[12] By the mid-1960's the term was widely used by students of individual political behavior and by students of general political systems.

THE POLITICAL SYSTEM AND THE INDIVIDUAL

Political socialization processes operate at both the individual and community levels. At the community level it is best understood as cultural transmission. Nations perpetuate their political standards by inducting new generations into established patterns of thought and action. We speak of "the American way of doing things." Majority rule, competitive elections, national loyalty, accepting the general rules of the game even when we dislike specific policies; all are part of "the American way." From one generation to the next these standards are passed on.

Political socialization also has to do with the way in which the individual acquires his political views. Most political socialization researchers have asked: Under the tutelage of what social agencies and through which social processes does the child form his "political self"? In this way, political socialization directs attention to the politically relevant learning experiences of the individual, for instance, how pledging allegiance to the flag each morning might stimulate a patriotic feeling in the school child.

These two perspectives — political socialization as cultural transmission and as individual learning — are complementary. Studies should proceed at both levels, each type of study drawing on the findings of the other. We do voice one warning, however. Undue emphasis on the question "how does a child become politically socialized" can hinder our understanding of more general political issues. Political scholars should guard

---

[12] Gabriel A. Almond, "A Functional Approach to Comparative Politics," in Gabriel A. Almond and James S. Coleman (eds.), *The Politics of the Developing Areas* (Princeton: Princeton University Press, 1960); Lucian W. Pye, "Political Modernization and Research on the Process of Political Socialization," *Items*, XIII (1959), pp. 25–28; and David Easton, "Problems in the Study of Political Socialization," Center for Advanced Study in the Behavioral Sciences and the University of Chicago, 1957, unpublished manuscript.

against letting their intellectual energies and research resources be drained into social-psychological queries, however
important the latter may be.

The payoff in political socialization theory is not with the
question posed as individual learning. More important are
questions about the consequences of political socialization
processes for the society. Issues of political violence, governmental deception, aggressive national behavior, social stagna-
tion, or racial injustice, will be better understood when we
have become more knowledgeable about political socialization.
Whether the future holds peaceful politics, honesty in government, international cooperation, social progress, and racial
tolerance is in part being answered in the classrooms,
churches, families, and youth groups of today. The next generation of citizens is being fashioned in the present.

CHAPTER II

The Political Self

POLITICAL SOCIALIZATION is a special form of the more general
phenomenon of socialization. We have explained that the concept of socialization has been borrowed in recent years from
other behavioral sciences, most notably from the cultural-
personality school of anthropology. Though its sources lie
there, it has not been adopted without considerable change.
Interested in explaining more peculiarly political phenomena,
political scientists have reformulated the concept so that it
better fits their theoretical interests. Understanding this re-
formulation is instructive in pointing to what occurs in political socialization.

Cultural anthropologists, who were among the first to study
socialization, were influenced greatly by Freudian assumptions.
These assumptions fashioned socialization analysis. Childhood
socialization — frequently referred to as child-rearing or
training — was viewed primarily as a mechanism through
which the child's "antisocial" tendencies were controlled.[1]
Civilized society is possible, the Freudians argue, only to the
extent that the child learns that he cannot replace his father,
marry his sister, take his neighbor's belongings, or engage in
other often tempting antisocial behavior. Society and its representatives, through their socialization mechanisms, suppress

[1] Much of this literature is reviewed by Irvin L. Child, "Socialization,"
in Gardner Lindzey (ed.), *Handbook of Social Psychology*, II (Reading,
Mass.: Addison-Wesley, 1954), pp. 655–692.

the child's "natural" tendencies. Socialization channels, constrains, limits, restricts, suppresses. Further, it helps the individual rationalize and justify the sacrifices he must make to join or become part of society. Socialization ushers the individual into society as it forces him to shed antisocial inclinations.

This interpretation of socialization was possibly the dominant theme in early cultural anthropology. But even for culture and personality students most taken with Freudian analysis, socialization came to involve other things as well. Field researchers point out that the child is developed as he is socialized. He is taught the technology of his society, is introduced to its cultural lore, is instructed in his rights as well as duties, and is engaged in a new world of social relationships. As George Herbert Mead wrote, "a self is formed."

We have then a dual process in socialization. On the one hand, socialization is the closing up of certain behavioral options. An initially wide range of alternatives becomes narrower as one is socialized. But on the other hand, socialization is to "make social" in such a way as to open up and develop, not only to constrain the self.

When political scientists adapted socialization theories to their interests they largely ignored the Freudian implications. It is interesting that none of the early studies of political socialization asked: "How does political socialization control the natural antipolitical predispositions of the child?" — a question most appropriate and consistent with early cultural-personality investigations. Rather it was asked: "How is the child introduced to his citizen roles, to the world of politics?" Political socialization has been viewed largely as opening up the world of politics for the individual. The emphasis has been upon how the child becomes emotionally attached to the political community and how he is provided with the information and predispositions appropriate to citizenship. Political socialization develops the citizen as it opens up a social world to the individual — the world of political allegiances and alliances, political rules and rituals, political personalities and policies, political symbols and behavior. This emphasis on political socialization as "introduction to" is a subtle, but important, break from the use to which the term was put by the earlier students of culture and personality from whom it was borrowed. We recognize, of course, that political socialization includes some negative and suppressive aspects. Behaviors which might be detrimental to the stability and well-being of the political community are inhibited. Acts of disloyalty, political vendettas, tax evasion are among those behaviors not viewed as options by the well socialized citizen.

For the most part, however, political socialization is the developmental process through which the citizen matures politically. The citizen acquires a complex of beliefs, feelings, and information which help him comprehend, evaluate, and relate to the political world around him. His political views are a part of his more general social views. As we shall see later, what the citizen feels about political life is distinct from and yet related to his religious, economic, and cultural views.

Adopting Mead's expression, we say that each individual has a *political self*. This term refers to his entire complex of orientations regarding his political world, including his views toward his own political role. In suggesting "political self" as a shorthand reference to an individual's package of orientations regarding politics, we are borrowing purposefully from Mead's notion of the social self.[2] Through his relationships with the social world an individual develops a political self. As Mead wrote of the more inclusive social self:

> The self is something which has a development; it is not initially there, at birth, but arises in the process of social experience and activity, that is, develops in the given individual as a result of his relations to that process as a whole and to other individuals within that process.[3]

Using this terminology, we suggest that political socialization produces a political self.

2 See George Herbert Mead, *Mind, Self, and Society* (Chicago: University of Chicago Press, 1934).

3 *Ibid.*, p. 135.

The attitudes, beliefs, and feelings citizens have regarding the political world are extremely diverse. It is difficult to envision a classification scheme that would encompass them all. As a preliminary notion, we suggest that political orientations have dimensions like these. They involve a little or a lot of information about the political world. They entail positive, negative, or neutral views. Involvement or identification with political symbols range from extremely strong to very weak. Individuals may expect anywhere from a great deal to practically nothing from the government in services, protection, or assurances. More concretely, an individual's political self is likely to include these: feelings of nationalism, patriotism, or tribal loyalty; identification with particular partisan factions or groups; attitudes and evaluations of specific political issues and personalities; knowledge regarding political structures and procedures; and a self-image of rights, responsibilities, and position in the political world.[4]

Not all individuals have political orientations; that is, not all individuals have developed a political self. The infant is the most obvious example. One is not born with an awareness of the political world, and indeed, does not develop much of an awareness for a number of years following birth. In addition, some adults living in social, geographic, or psychological isolation from the rest of society may never develop a political self. At the most they will have only a partially formulated one. All societies have persons who exist at their fringe. These people have only limited interactions with other citizens. They are relatively ignorant about the society and its components. Some awareness of the political world on the part of an individual is a minimal requirement for the existence of a political self. Notions about the political world may be correct or in-

[4] In their comparative analysis of political cultures in five nations Almond and Verba develop a classification scheme for political orientations based on the various aspects of the political system toward which orientations are directed. Their scheme includes both levels of the system and a variety of functions of the system. They use their scheme as a basis for talking about different types of political cultures. We are not interested here in the development of such a rigorous scheme, but rather in presenting some notion of the variety of important political orientations. See Gabriel Almond and Sidney Verba, *The Civic Culture* (Princeton: Princeton University Press, 1963), pp. 3–42.

correct, pro or con. The distortion may be great. For the moment we are not concerned with the quality of political orientations. Our point is that unless a person is at least aware of political objects of one type or another, we cannot speak of his having political orientations, or a political self.

The political self, then, is made — not born. Political maturation is a process through which a person without a political self begins to acquire and subsequently to develop complex and varied political orientations. It is political socialization which molds and shapes the citizen's relationship to the political community. Part of this process can be seen as taking general predispositions of the child and directing them toward political objects. An orphan, for example, shunted from one institution to another or from one foster parent to another may learn to mistrust older persons. He discovers that adults, especially those with authority, often behave in very capricious ways. At the same time the orphan is deprived of the security and love characteristic of most parent-child relationships. The child becomes cynical and mistrustful. This general predisposition is not a political orientation, however. It becomes "political" only when he encounters political authorities. As an adolescent the orphan may well view the policeman with suspicion; as an adult he is likely to doubt whether government officials are as benevolent as they claim. It is when his cynicism becomes attached to political objects that his general social view becomes part of his political self.

Acquiring a political self is a natural corollary to general social maturation. As with all social learning, political learning is gradual and incremental. There is no magic point in youth when the "political self" is suddenly acquired. Each citizen's political views result from lifelong experiences. Political socialization is the gradual molding of the political self. A convenient way of explaining how political maturation occurs is to distinguish between different orientations acquired by the citizen. We suggest three very broad categories. Though not an exhaustive or perfect classification by any means, this categorization does impose some meaningful order on our discussion.

1. The basic foundation of the political self includes political attachments and loyalties.[5] These feelings, often very intense, are directed toward the nation — "I am an American" — or toward significant political symbols — "communism is the best form of government." Also included are views toward groups and social categories which take on political meaning and thus shape the political self: "White supremacy" or "black power" illustrates such basic interpretive orientations.

2. In a somewhat less basic way, various forms of specific knowledge about and feelings toward political institutions are part of the political self. To recognize and appreciate that federalism is part of the United States constitutional order is of this intermediate level.

3. Finally, a citizen has more transient views which nevertheless are part of his political self. He reacts to specific political policies, programs, personalities, and events. To support a presidential candidate or to favor a legislative act may be less basic than a patriotic identification with the nation and it may be less basic than an appreciation of federalism, but such orientations still contribute to a person's "political self."

The advantage of this scheme is that it links political socialization experiences to stages of the maturation process. For the most part, political socialization studies have been limited to listing political socialization agencies on one side of a ledger and a mass of undifferentiated political orientations on the other. A developmental profile permits more refined hypotheses. We can hypothesize, for instance, that early acquired basic orientations such as national loyalty are learned by imitation in the family. Other facets of the political self are formed later in life and in response to different socialization agents.

We can make the three categories more understandable with a few illustrations. The earliest and, under normal conditions, most durable political orientation a child acquires is his

[5] Clifford Geertz uses the term "primordial sentiments" to describe much the same phenomena. See his "The Integrative Revolution: Primordial Sentiments and Civic Politics in the New States," in Clifford Geertz (ed.), *Old Societies and New States: The Quest for Modernity in Asia and Africa* (New York: The Free Press, 1963), pp. 105–157. Our usage is also similar to Verba's notion of basic political values.

identification with his political community. Very young children the world over know to what nation they belong. This identification is often accompanied by a strong sense of loyalty. The five-year-old French child says "I am French and France is the best country in the world. The tricolor is my flag and I feel excited when I see it." Neither the national goals nor the political institutions of France will be at all clear to this five-year-old. His intense attachment is independent of any detailed knowledge about France. He is likely to be completely ignorant of his country's history and will have, at best, only a vague knowledge of national boundaries and even of who else belongs to the political community. However little content the child's attachment may have, it nonetheless is developed early and seems to serve a very basic need to belong.

This point is carefully documented in an extensive study of American grade school children. Two of the scholars connected with this research interpret their findings as follows:

> The young child's involvement with the political system begins with a strong positive attachment to the country; the U.S. is seen as ideal and as superior to other countries. This attachment to the country is stable and shows almost no change through elementary school years. This bond is possibly the most basic and essential aspect of socialization into involvement with the political life of the nation. Essentially an emotional tie, it apparently grows from complex psychological and social needs and is exceedingly resistant to change or argument. . . .[6]

A critical facet of "learning to be loyal" merits brief notice here, and more extended discussion in the final chapter. At the same time as the child is acquiring his sense of loyalty, he is also being taught the virtues of obedience. More to the point, he learns to be loyal *and* to be compliant from the same people — teachers and parents. For the child, loyalty to authorities and obedience to authorities are not easily distinguished. Goodness equals compliance. In the same way, children learn

[6] Robert D. Hess and Judith V. Torney, *The Development of Political Attitudes in Children* (Chicago: Aldine Publishing Co., 1967), p. 213.

to express their loyalty to the political order by obeying its laws. Insofar as loyalty — that strong and persistent sense of attachment to the state — is a major component of the political self, it is likely that the political self will be characterized by a sense of the appropriateness of obedience.

At about the same time the child is learning loyalty and obedience to the political state, he is also developing attachments to other important political symbols. He may, for example, identify with socialism, communism, or democracy. At the early age at which the child becomes aware of these symbols, the meaning of them as ideologies or forms of government will not be clear. Like the early ties with the nation-state, they are very emotional and yet somewhat vague. In the United States the child is likely to identify himself with one of the major political parties. But the child's sense that he is a "Democrat" or a "Republican" is not associated with policy preferences. That comes later.

As he acquires basic loyalties and identifications with political symbols, the child learns to sort people into social categories — linguistic, racial, class, tribal, occupational, or geographical. In large part, socialization is teaching a child the "social category system." Children learn to classify people according to certain characteristics and to behave differently toward them depending on how they are classified. Further, the child identifies with those categories to which he belongs. He adopts behavior appropriate to being white rather than colored, Gentile rather than Jewish, a Kikuyu rather than a Luo, first-generation rather than fifth-generation, and so forth. Learning his society's category system and identifying with particular categories are not in themselves political orientations. They do serve as important reference and interpretation points. A child's sense of belonging to one rather than another social group is the basis for important perspectives regarding the political world.

Not only are basic identifications and loyalties the earliest acquired by the child, they are also among the strongest and the most resistant to change in later life. It is remarkable to witness the endurance of nationalism, group identifications, and partisan loyalties, even in the face of extensive pressure toward change. The persistence of basic views is of great importance for the overall development of the political self. These feelings serve as the foundation upon which subsequently acquired orientations are built. Political events and experiences later in life are interpreted within the context of these basic orientations. They serve as "political eyeglasses," through which the individual perceives and makes meaningful the world of politics. The child, for example, may acquire strong emotional attachments to an institution such as the Catholic Church, an ideological position such as socialism, or a political symbol such as republicanism. These attachments guide his later interpretation of and reaction to more concrete political happenings, such as choosing between government leaders or public policies. They also condition the political roles he will fashion for himself — whether he will be an activist or an isolate, an extremist or a moderate, and so forth.

In more advanced childhood and early youth, the individual begins to fill in these vague attachments and identifications with more precise knowledge and information. Political symbols assume more specific shapes and characteristics.[7] Democracy is no longer just a vague symbol but one which specifically connotes competitive elections and control of political authorities by constitutional means. The individual learns how his political world is structured and where he fits into it. Government officials are elected and he, the citizen, gets to cast his ballot along with everyone else. Identifications with political parties or other partisan groups begin to take on ideological meaning. The attachment to the Republican Party gradually includes specific policy positions on welfare legislation or taxation issues. A general predisposition toward political participation is broadened to include knowledge about the forms of petition available to the average citizen.

The political self is never "finalized." A citizen is confronted continuously with new political configurations and events. He is faced with choices about new political candidates. Different public policies and governmental activities will attract his at-

[7] This aspect of political learning is discussed by David Easton and Jack Dennis in, "The Child's Image of Government," *The Annals*, CCCLXI (September 1965), pp. 40–57.

tention as he ages. Political orientations formed in the 1930's are only partially relevant in the 1960's. The last thirty years have witnessed a shift of government power from the states to the central government, a shift from laissez-faire economics to managed fiscal policy, a shift from isolationism to internationalism and even interventionism.

Attitudes toward specific policies and personalities are, on the whole, less strongly held than general political loyalties and attachments. The more concrete and specific orientations however, are conditioned — though not determined by — earlier acquired and more intensely held values. The patriot of the 1930's might well have been an isolationist; the same person, thirty years later, might support his government just as strongly when it engaged in police action halfway around the globe. His basic loyalty doesn't waver; his specific policy position alters completely, however.

We suggest that the development of political orientations is cumulative. Early orientations greatly influence later acquisitions. The range of beliefs, information, and attitudes one adopts in later life are limited by early political learning. The development of strong attachments to a particular political or social grouping will tend to prescribe one set of political choices and experiences, and to delimit others. Selective perceptivity by the individual helps assure that the basic labels and identifications acquired early are not drastically challenged in later life.

The patterns suggested here, of course, are merely approximate. Political learning is less rigid and firmly set than this. Under some circumstances fundamental political loyalties developed in early childhood may be abandoned, and new basic attachments may develop late in life. Attachments to symbols encountered in adult life may take on greater importance for an individual than his primary orientations. Nonetheless, we believe that this conceptualization provides a rough, generally applicable classification of political orientations and of the general structure through which they are acquired and developed. We shall use this classification as we discuss the process of political socialization and the agencies through which it is carried out.

CHAPTER III

The Political Culture

A VISITOR TO ANOTHER COUNTRY, especially if he has been observant and inquisitive, will often return home to report that "politics sure are different there; they don't do things as we do." Assume that the traveler is just back from Central America. He might say something like this. "Seems like every time there is a political difference, someone gets killed. People kept assuring me they had democracy, but no one put much faith in elections. The newspapers were full of stories about corruption. I talked to cab drivers and clerks and barbers and people like that every time I got a chance. They seemed agreed that a revolution is what was needed, but then few of them thought it would change the way things were going. At least in the United States we make a pretense of treating Negroes equally. The wealthy people I spoke with did not even pretend that the peasant farmer deserved political equality. Just for fun I attended a political rally and was really surprised to see bodyguards surrounding all the speakers."

This traveler has engaged in "cross-cultural" comparisons. He knows that politics at home and politics in Central America have some striking differences. In the language we will use, the Central American "political culture" is unlike that of North America. The tourist noticed that violence was an accepted political weapon, that adherence to the democratic creed did not include faith in elections, that revolution rather than reform was the expected response to a corrupt government, that the man on the street approached politics with fatalistic resignation, that elitist values were shared by the wealthy, and that political leaders feared even their own followers. He refers, in concrete words, to the political style, values, norms, and behavior patterns of the society as a whole. He recognizes that a nation has a distinct "political culture."

The phrase "political culture" summarizes a complex and varied portion of social reality. Among other things, a nation's political culture includes political traditions and folk heroes, the spirit of public institutions, political passions of the citizenry, goals articulated by the political ideology, and both formal and informal rules of the political game. It also includes other real, but elusive, factors, such as political stereotypes, political style, political moods, the tone of political exchanges, and finally, some sense of what is appropriately political and what is not.

Scholars interested in analyzing the relationship between the structure and operation of polities and the peculiar culture in which they operate have developed and defined the concept of political culture more rigorously. Almond, in his important 1956 essay on "Comparative Political Systems," pointed out that "every political system is embedded in a particular pattern of orientations to political actions." [1] This pattern of orientations he labeled the system's "political culture." In a similar vein, Lucian Pye has referred to the political culture as "the ordered subjective realm of politics." [2] This notion of the political culture has been succinctly captured by Sidney Verba. He writes:

> [Political culture] refers to the system of beliefs about patterns of political interaction and political institutions. It refers not to what is happening in the world of politics, but what people believe about those happenings. And these beliefs can be of several kinds: they can be empirical beliefs about what the actual state of political life is; they can be beliefs as to the goals or

[1] Gabriel A. Almond, "Comparative Political Systems," *Journal of Politics,* XVIII (1956), p. 396.

[2] Lucian W. Pye, "Introduction: Political Culture and Political Development," in Lucian W. Pye and Sidney Verba (eds.), *Political Culture and Political Development* (Princeton: Princeton University Press, 1965), p. 7.

values that ought to be pursued in political life; and these beliefs may have an important expressive or emotional dimension.[3]

Political culture, conceptualized roughly, is the pattern of distribution of orientations members of a political community have toward politics.[4] This patterned collectivity of orientations influences the structure, operation, and stability of political life.[5]

Political socialization shapes and transmits a nation's political culture. More specifically, political socialization *maintains* a nation's political culture insofar as it transmits that culture from old to new constituents. It *transforms* the political culture insofar as it leads the population, or parts of it, to view and experience politics differently from the way in which they did previously. Under exaggerated change or special occasions, such as the bringing into existence of a new political community, we might even say that political socialization processes *create* a political culture where none had existed before.

These three terms — "maintaining," "transforming," and "creating" — summarize the variety of tasks political socialization performs for the political culture. Under stable conditions political socialization will maintain over time the population's basic attachments and orientations toward politics. This is accomplished by assuring that the identifications and orientations are transmitted successfully from one generation to the next. Statistically speaking, stable social and political conditions are not the norm in the contemporary world. A majority of the nations are engaged rather in transforming old and creating new political structures and social arrangements. Nation-building tasks include developing an "attitude dimension" or "subjective realm" compatible with new structural and institutional arrangements. The question of whether the basic influence of political socialization at any particular time is that of maintaining and transmitting an existing politi-

[3] Sidney Verba, "Comparative Political Culture," in Pye and Verba, *ibid.*, p. 516.

[4] See Gabriel A. Almond and Sidney Verba, *The Civic Culture* (Princeton: Princeton University Press, 1963), especially Chapter I.

[5] This notion is the basic rationale of Pye and Verba, *loc. cit.*

cal culture, replacing or transforming an older one, or creating a new one in a new society, depends upon several factors. The history of the country, the pressures of the social and international environment, the appropriateness of traditional outlooks toward political life, and the goals, aims, and purposes of leaders and citizens, all are relevant.

These three tasks are not, of course, mutually exclusive and unambiguous categories for describing how political socialization affects various polities. More accurately, they suggest a continuum. At one pole of the continuum, each successive generation perfectly replicates the political culture of the preceding generation. At the other pole, there is no continuity from one point in history to the next. Neither of these extremes will be found in the real world. There is no society in which political socialization processes involve solely maintaining, transforming, or creating, in the pure meaning of these terms. Any society has a mixture. The real world is composed of countries in which political socialization agencies are simultaneously protecting certain traditions, transforming other aspects of the political culture, and creating new values appropriate to new political conditions.

Post-World War II Germany and revolutionary Russia are examples of nations whose leaders have engaged in deliberate programs of transforming traditional national cultures, as part of the establishment of a new social and political order. In Germany the effort has been directed at developing more democratic orientations.[6] Both the allied occupational forces and the postwar German government have attempted to reshape German political values and attitudes to make them correspond with democratic political structures. The Soviet government, since 1917, has engaged in an extensive attempt to transform a traditional Russian political culture. In this instance, the goal has been to encourage orientations more in keeping with their blueprints for a socialist state. Mainland China and the nations of Eastern Europe are currently engaged in operations not too dissimilar from those of the Soviet Union.

[6] See Sidney Verba, "Germany: The Remaking of Political Culture," in Pye and Verba, *ibid.*, pp. 130–170.

The newly independent nations in Africa and Asia have been faced with even more fundamental and difficult tasks in regard to their respective political cultures.[7] These nations, often, have had to create or develop a common political culture — oriented toward the new nation and its structures and processes — where previously there was none. Peoples without a common political culture or common political history have been put together in new national entities. One of the most crucial socialization tasks for the leadership and machinery has been directing political loyalties toward that new national unit.

At the opposite end of the continuum, in countries with long political histories and relatively stable political institutions and populations, political socialization mechanisms transmit political orientations from one generation to another. If we can assume that over time the stable system has developed a political culture made up of political orientations "appropriate" to that political order, we expect to find, not new orientations, but the old ones perpetuated. The United States and most Western European nations approximate this condition in the contemporary world. Of course, as we have remarked, in no ongoing polity will we find that changes or adjustments in the political culture are not occurring. Adjustments are constantly being made to new or changing policies, programs, leadership. A more extensive statement of what takes place with regard to each of these tasks will help elaborate what political socialization does.

MAINTAINING THE POLITICAL CULTURE

The clearest instance of how the political socialization process maintains the political culture is the propensity of the older generation for passing on its political values, views, norms, and beliefs to the children of the society. As captured in the eloquent words of the United States Supreme Court:

> The ultimate foundation of a free society is the binding tie of cohesive sentiment. Such a sentiment is fostered by all those

[7] James S. Coleman, "The Political Systems of the Developing Areas," in Almond and Coleman, *The Politics of the Developing Areas* (Princeton: Princeton University Press, 1960), pp. 532–576.

agencies of the mind and spirit which may serve to gather up
the traditions of a people, transmit them from generation to
generation, and thereby, create that continuity of a treasured
common life which constitutes a civilization.[8]

In the language we employ, "gathering up" and "transmitting" the "traditions of the people" is equivalent to political
socialization maintaining a political culture by acquainting
the young with the political values of their parents. Such transmission is important in all ongoing societies, whether classified
as free or not. Through those agencies shaping the "mind and
spirit" — the family, the schools, churches, youth groups —
the collective political culture is transmitted from one generation to the next. This sort of transgenerational transmission of
common political values is the heart of political socialization
as generally conceived.

Political socialization as transmission may be more or less
institutional and coordinated. In the United States the political culture is transmitted from parent to child, from teacher
to student, from den mother to cub scout, in a relatively
haphazard and uncoordinated fashion. There is no central
institution to oversee the entire process. There is no way to
guarantee that all children will be similarly informed about
the adult political positions they will some day fill. Certain so-
called "totalitarian" societies have been more self-conscious
about transmitting political information and values to the
young, and have attempted to coordinate and regulate such
activities. Hitler's Youth League and the Young Pioneers of
the Soviet Union are examples of programmed and manipulated agents of political socialization.

Puberty rites in many preindustrial societies illustrate very
clearly how the parent generation controls entry into adult
roles.[9] These rites initiate the young into the rights, responsibilities, and mysteries of adulthood. They do this in part by
systematically divesting the adolescent of youthful characteristics. There is strict separation of the adult world from that
of the child. The Masai boy, armed only with a spear, tradi-

[8] *Minersville School District vs. Gobitis* (310 U.S. 506, 1940).
[9] S. N. Eisenstadt, *From Generation to Generation* (New York: The
Free Press, 1956), Chapter I.

tionally has been required to kill a lion to claim adult status. Killing the lion permits the male youth to participate in the symbolic ritual activities which inform him of the tribal lore, the behavior appropriate to his new status, and the duties of adulthood. Puberty rites illustrate socialization as the passing of cultural values from one generation to the next in its most ritual and exaggerated form. Bar mitzvahs, Boy Scout ceremonies, public school graduations are equivalents in our culture.

Children probably are the largest and most important group which need to be socialized if a political culture is to be maintained, but they are not the only group. Other "new members" frequently are socialized into citizen roles by older members. Immigrants often absorb the cultural values of their new homeland. During the late 1800's and early 1900's the public schools in the United States were an important political socialization agency for large numbers of Europeans who immigrated to the growing urban-industrial centers. In spite of the efforts of the Know-Nothings to preserve the "purity" of America, both public and private agencies transmitted to these new arrivals and to their offspring the sense of being "American." Among the immigrant families the normal pattern of parents socializing children was reversed. It was often the children who transmitted the American culture to their elders. The children began to learn the norms and operations of American democracy in the schools, and returned home to tell them to parents and grandparents. In the contemporary world, Israel stands out as a nation pressed to pass on a newly developing political culture to large numbers of immigrants. Other examples of political socialization maintaining the political culture as it transmits information, traditions, and beliefs from generation to generation, or from established members of society to newcomers, will come up in various contexts throughout this book.

TRANSFORMING THE POLITICAL CULTURE

What people believe about politics is generally kept in some more or less compatible relationship with what is actually happening in the political world. Self-adjusting mechanisms as well as deliberate plans continually adjust the political culture, marginally or radically, to correspond to changing conditions. Because nations are almost always experiencing some types of change, political socialization mechanisms are constantly pressed to make alterations in the political culture. In some instances such alterations are only minor; in others, they entail extensive changes. Sometimes the political orientations of an entire population are affected. Sometimes it is only a subgroup of the population whose political beliefs are undergoing change. As we suggested above, postwar Germany and the Soviet Union are recent examples of nations whose leaders have set out deliberately to bring about great changes in the political culture.

Events in the United States following the Constitutional Convention of 1787 also clearly exemplify a political culture being transformed as a result of substantial modification of the political regime. Replacing the Articles of Confederation with the Constitution fundamentally rearranged the relationship of citizen to government and of governmental unit to governmental unit. Prior to 1787, the central government had no social control over individuals. It could neither tax, arrest, imprison, nor induct them into the armed services. After the Constitution was modified, the population had to be informed of far-reaching changes. Further, the citizens adjusted their orientations so as to offer some support to the new authorities and arrangements. Old allegiances and loyalties to the states were altered, and new loyalties to the nation developed. Part of what had been learned about politics was forgotten and new information took its place. The political culture was transformed as opinion leaders, schools, churches, mass media, and political groups began to instruct the population with respect to the new political order. These types of transformation were not rare in the past and still occur in the contemporary political world.

Changes in the political structure are not the only factors calling for transformation of the political culture. Alterations in the social stratification system, the economic structures, the religious beliefs, and the international arena can, each in its own way, call forth changes in the political culture. Political socialization agencies are responsive to such changes. These agencies, in introducing new norms and orientations into an existing political culture, alter its content.

Sometimes it is a subgroup of the population which is transformed politically. Geographic isolates frequently develop a political culture unlike the one which characterizes the remainder of society — e.g., the American South, French Canada, the Highlands of Scotland. Another category of frequent isolates is formed by those who occupy the lower rungs of the socioeconomic stratification system. Shut off from the major avenues of political information and participation, they frequently develop a political culture quite unlike that of the more prosperous, politically active middle and upper classes. In the United States the American Indians and the Negroes, particularly the southern rural Negroes, are social and geographic isolates. The peasantry, nomadic tribes, and mountain dwellers of many parts of the world are isolates having differentiated cultures. A widespread contemporary phenomenon is the integration of many of these isolates into national, often "urban and industrial," cultures. There is considerable pressure from the elites of new nations to transform traditional subcultures.

The problems associated with distinct subcultures are well illustrated by the urban riots in the United States. The ghetto Negro is becoming both more political and more radical. The "Black Power" political culture includes goals and values quite alien to the dominant white middle-class emphasis on orderly change, residential segregation, and gentlemanly — however unjust — politics. Black Power advocates refuse to be absorbed into a dominant culture which will divest them of their political strength. They long ago learned that to fight with the political weapons sanctioned by City Hall spells frustration and eventual defeat. Their response has been to fashion other political weapons, and in so doing, to introduce new political values. The American political culture will be very much affected by how urban tension is handled. Some commentators fear a resurgence of political suppression, partly in response to Negro riots and partly resulting from the free-floating anxiety caused by the prolonged fighting in Asia.

We have reviewed a few of the conditions involving substantial transformations in political cultures and subcultures. The reader should keep in mind that political socialization processes in every society are at least partially transforming the political culture at all times. As political policies and programs change, people's experiences with the political order change. We can expect alterations of political views accordingly. A war, a depression, urban riots, an invasion, a coup, a shift in international alliances, and so forth, all rearrange the political order and consequently transform the political culture. Political socialization agencies mediate between the changes in the political-social order and alterations in the political culture.

CREATING A POLITICAL CULTURE

Some new nations are political entities without a history. The people who suddenly find themselves members of the same political community — in a de jure if not de facto sense — may not share a common language, culture, history, religion, or enemy. Some of the new African states are the most exaggerated examples of this strange political phenomenon. During the nineteenth century the French, Belgians, Germans, British, and Portuguese portioned out territories in Africa with little regard for pre-existing political boundaries. Several tribal or kingdom units were assigned arbitrarily to common political units. In administering these "protectorates" or "colonies," the European powers depended more on coercion than on developing supportive cultural norms. The colonial administrator generally demonstrated little interest in encouraging the growth of a sentiment of national cohesion or for integrating disparate elements within the common administrative unit.

In recent years there has been a transition from colonial control to independence, and the leaders of the new nations have been called upon to govern geographical areas which have no heritage of national integration, no common political culture; indeed, the opposite has often been true. For example, the tribes, linguistic groups, and kingdoms brought together under one government in Uganda have a long history of bitter competition and conflict. On the West Coast of

Africa, Nigeria is a similar case. The inability of postindependence leadership to integrate the Ibos, Hausas, and Yorubas into one political unit has led to violence, civil war, and the possible creation of a new state, Biafra.

Leaders of new nations are trying not only to create economic and political institutions, they also are spending much energy attempting to create appropriate cultural values. The Prime Minister of Uganda, Milton Obote, addressed Uganda primary school teachers as follows:

> Our reconstruction of national education must . . . aim at creating a unity of purpose among all our nationals, and developing in them a common outlook which will transcend and harmonize in an attractive pattern the differences in history, background, language and culture that exist among various sections of the people.[10]

Uganda shares with other new nations the lack of a general, systematic pattern of political norms which can be adopted by the average citizen. Let us again use George Herbert Mead's phrase: there is no political "generalized other." New nations have yet to evolve a way in which to view and evaluate political matters. Traditional values — loyalty to the tribe, deference to the traditional leaders, old ways of farming — stand in some tension to modern values. Socialization agencies are marshaled, frequently under the control of a dominant political party, to the task of instilling suitable citizenship values, national patriotism, obedience to constitutional authorities, and commitment to modern economic techniques.

Under conditions rather common in the mid-twentieth century, political socialization agencies attempt to generate new political cultures. But, just as no political culture is maintained intact, creation never occurs without integration and maintenance of old values with the new. As Uganda's

---

[10] From a speech delivered by Obote to the Annual Conference of the Uganda Educational Association, August 14, 1963, Jinja, Uganda. For a more general treatment of creating political culture in a new nation, see Kenneth Prewitt and Joseph Okello-Oculi, "Political Education and Political Socialization in New Nations," Roberta Sigel (ed.), *Learning about Politics: Studies in Political Socialization* (New York: Random House, forthcoming).

Prime Minister urged, the "common outlook" should "harmonize" as well as transcend the divergent histories. Even the newest nations of the world manage to build political cultures which absorb important elements from the past.

SUMMARY

From one perspective, it is useful to define political socialization as the process which provides the individual with his political self as he advances through childhood, adolescence, and adulthood. In general, the citizen acquires basic political loyalties and identifications at a fairly early age, more specific understanding of political events and happenings a little later, and orientations and reactions to political policies and personalities as he encounters them in adult life.

From a second perspective, political socialization transmits and shapes the political culture of the nation as a whole. Older generations leave their mark on the politics of the future by communicating to their children how the political game is to be played. Previous ways of doing things in the political realm are encoded into the "political memory" of a nation. The political memory is transmitted through the political socialization process. In any society, political socialization will be maintaining some cultural values, transforming others, and introducing yet others. When a country falls primarily into one category, as many do, its political socialization practices will reflect this. The collective political life of the nation will be relatively stable, or will be undergoing marginal alterations, or will be experiencing changes of a revolutionary magnitude. Whichever occurs, political socialization agencies will be the bearers of the cultural values.

PART II

Processes

POLITICAL SOCIALIZATION, like other forms of social learning, is a series of social and psychological processes. It occurs as individuals meet and mix with other persons and respond to the symbols and institutions of society. Man comes into the world with certain biological characteristics and potentialities. Among the more important of his potentialities is the ability to relate emotionally with other humans; to form the relationships that are the basis of human society. As Aristotle has instructed us, man is not born or reared in isolation from other men. He is "born into" an ongoing society with existing structures, norms, and patterns of behavior. Immediately upon birth man begins to interact with that society — with parents, brothers and sisters, playmates, relatives, teachers.

Socialization is one element of the relationships between an individual and his society. From the perspective of society, socialization involves transmitting values and behavioral patterns to the individual. In doing this, socialization agencies force the individual to abandon some types of behavior and urge him to adopt others. In Western culture the child learns that he should not appear in public unclothed. He is urged to walk and talk as early as possible. From the individual's side of the exchange, socialization entails the development and shaping of his abilities and potential so that he fits into his society. Socialization entails established social patterns on the one hand, and persons with the capacity to acquire social knowledge and attachments on the other.

To understand socialization it is necessary to take account of both these elements. Lack of adequate physical or mental faculties can keep an individual from being socialized. Temporarily, all children lack the faculties to participate fully in the adult social world. Individuals with given mental and physical potentials will develop differently in varying social arrangements. Winston Churchill, George Bernard Shaw, and Bertrand Russell would not have become towering world statesman, playwright, and philosopher, if they had been taken at birth to an isolated Eskimo village or a South Pacific island, and remained there in isolation from Western culture.

Political socialization takes place as the individual has social experiences that lead to relationships with the world of politics. These experiences constitute the developmental process through which he acquires his political self. We use the word "acquire" here to stress the interactive nature of socialization. The individual is not altogether passive in his socialization, nor is he the sole acting or initiating agent. Definitions of socialization that employ notions such as "enculturation," "building in," "induction," etc., imply too passive a role for the individual. Terms such as "learns" and "adapts himself," on the other hand, place too much emphasis on an active or initiating part for the individual being socialized. Such terms underemphasize the influence of the socializing agents. The reality of the socialization process lies between these two extremes.

Individuals both "socialize themselves" and "are socialized." Different types of socialization experiences may lean more toward one extreme than the other. In some instances the individual is more passive. Most early childhood political socialization is of this variety. Children often pick up values about political institutions and leaders without active interest or initiative on their part. Cues for political values or preferences are dropped unintentionally by adults, and the child often unconsciously picks them up merely from overhearing adult conversations. In other instances the individual takes more initiative, and the socializing agent is more passive.

"Anticipatory socialization" is of this form. Sometimes an individual anticipates a role he wants or expects to assume in the future and begins to take on characteristics associated with that role long before he actually achieves the position. The premedical student and the prelaw student begin to think and act like doctors and lawyers even before they get to medical school or law school. The undergraduate student aspiring to become a political scientist may adopt the "liberal" political orientations of his political science teachers as he anticipates becoming a professional political scientist. In these instances the individual takes the initiative in seeking out and taking on selected characteristics.

These examples stress the extremes. Most political socialization experiences fall between these poles. Political socialization is a process in which both the individual and the agencies of socialization play parts.

The social and psychological experiences contributing to political socialization are numerous and varied. Political orientations may be acquired as a result of lessons or messages which have explicit political content, or they may be formed by picking up general predispositions which later become directed toward politics. A citizen's political views may result from explicit attempts by others to teach political principles, or they may be acquired as a side effect of experiences whose explicit intention is something quite different. Mass political rallies, election campaigns, and government propaganda are examples of direct and explicit socialization; so are attempts to teach knowledge about political life in the school curriculum. A son picking up his political party identification through overhearing his father and mother discussing politics, and a man deciding to vote because he has heard men at work arguing about candidates are examples of less direct political socialization. In the latter cases, social settings whose primary purposes are something other than political influence individual political orientations without intentionally attempting to do so.

Developments and alterations in political orientations take place through both individual experiences and common societal experiences. Much of political socialization is the passing on of knowledge, feelings, and values about politics through families, peer groups, schools, secondary groups, etc. The individuals of a society are socialized into the roles and norms of their political community. Though many individuals are going through similar processes, these are basically individual experiences.

Sometimes whole societies simultaneously go through experiences which affect the political views of the citizenry. Wars, economic crises, internal revolutions, the achievement of political independence are very sudden, wide-scale events which rapidly and generally alter political perspectives. The decisive defeats of the German Reich and of Japan in 1945 are particularly good examples. These defeats shattered expectations and aspirations of entire national populations and necessitated widespread changes in political outlooks. Other societal events change political orientations as thoroughly, but not as immediately, as these types of events. Industrialization, urbanization, and the expansion of political participation to new groups are examples of such conditions. These developments take place over a long period of time, but nonetheless alter substantially political orientations in their wake.

In the three chapters of this section on the processes of political socialization we discuss three major issues. In Chapter IV we outline the development of the political self as it takes place through the individual lifespan, the process of political maturation. In Chapter V we outline and differentiate the mechanisms of political learning. In the final chapter of the section we shift to the question of continuity and discontinuity in political socialization.

Age and the Development of the Political Self

POLITICAL SOCIALIZATION IS LIFELONG AND DEVELOPMENTAL

Among the most significant questions about political socialization is: how does it fit into the individual life cycle. At what age does political learning begin? How long does the process take? At what age, if any, can one say that it is completed or identify the fully developed political self? Related questions require that we define the types of political learning likely to occur during different periods in the life cycle. Is there a general pattern of political maturation?

Conventional wisdom as well as historical and contemporary social theory have emphasized the early childhood years as critical for developing personality, social attitudes, and cultural values. The adage that "the child is father to the man" expresses this notion. As a social institution the Catholic Church has long claimed that if it were permitted to influence the first seven years of a child's life the world could little alter his basic character and loyalties thereafter. Contemporary anthropologists and psychiatrists, concerned with the development of personality and values, have focused on child rearing practices and other very early experiences as major antecedents of personality and social character.[1] Social learning theorists

[1] See, for example, John W. M. Whiting and Irvin L. Child, *Child Training and Personality* (New Haven: Yale University Press, 1953).

similarly stress the importance of learning experiences in early childhood.[2] A wide array of evidence from recent studies of human behavior justifies the emphasis upon early experiences as a major aspect of socialization.

Political observers from the time of Plato have been sensitive to the consequences of childhood training for the political order. In *The Republic* Plato pointed out how important learning during early childhood is for preparing citizens with appropriate social and political values and impulses.[3] Tocqueville succinctly stated this notion in analyzing the social and cultural basis of American politics. He pointed out that to understand human character:

> We must begin higher up; we must watch the infant in his mother's arms; we must see the first images which the external world casts upon the dark mirror of his mind, the first occurrences that he witnesses; we must hear the first words which awaken the sleeping powers of thought, and stand by his earliest efforts if we would understand the prejudices, the habits, and the passions which will later rule his life. The entire man is, so to speak, to be seen in the cradle of the child.[4]

The term "socialization" sometimes is used exclusively for processes and experiences that take place during childhood. The assumption underlying this conception is that the social self not only develops early in childhood, but that once the individual passes through early socializing stages his "social development" is completed, his social self is formed. For our purposes, this assumption is misleading, though it is useful to emphasize the childhood period.

It is more accurate to view political socialization as a process that continues throughout the life span. Some types of political orientations, if not constantly changing, are susceptible to alteration even through adulthood and old age. The political self is continually developing. At no time can one say that an

[2] See, for example, Neal M. Miller and John Dollard, *Social Learning and Imitation* (New Haven: Yale University Press, 1941).

[3] Plato, *The Republic,* translated by Francis MacDonald Cornford (New York: Oxford University Press, 1956), Chapter 9.

[4] Alexis de Tocqueville, *Democracy in America,* Vol. I (New York: Vintage Books, 1945), pp. 27–28.

individual has been completely socialized or that his political self cannot be altered.

Though socialization is continuous, some periods in the life cycle are more important for political learning than others. Thus, the emphasis upon childhood experiences is not without justification. The experiences and developments that contribute most to the acquisition of political orientations are concentrated in the early years. This is especially true of basic political loyalties, identifications, and values.

In Chapter II we identified three types of political orientations; now we are ready to fit them into an age-developmental pattern of political socialization. In early childhood one acquires Type One basic identifications and emotional ties with political symbols, as well as finding out something about social groupings. This is the substance of early childhood political learning. In later childhood the child begins to acquire Type Two orientations: he understands what the nation is and acquires knowledge about its dimensions and expectations. Now he begins to map out the political universe around him and to discover where he fits into it. As the individual takes on various roles or positions in the political world throughout later life, he acquires Type Three orientations: a vast array of attitudes toward specific political personalities, activities, and policies. Political learning continues throughout life and follows a roughly sequential development. The types of political learning taking place at various stages in the life cycle are different.

Political learning is cumulative. Orientations learned early in life determine much of the form and substance of orientations acquired later. Political attachments acquired early both open up the possibility for some types of later learning and limit the likelihood that other types will occur. The youth who has acquired an interest in politics is more likely to be influenced by political events and to establish opinions on political happenings than the youth who has no such interest. The political interest acquired early in life sets the stage for exposure to and influence by socialization agents in later life. Early identification with a political party or societal grouping, such as a social class, may close the individual off from certain political stimuli and ideas in later life. By becoming attached to a socialist party at an early age, the European child effectively limits the likelihood of influence by nonsocialist political attitudes and values. These developmental patterns will become clearer as we examine childhood, adolescent, and adult political learning.

POLITICAL LEARNING DURING
CHILDHOOD AND YOUTH [5]

Political learning has its beginning early.[6] By the time they have reached social adulthood, individuals normally have fairly well formed political selves. By the late teens or early twenties, the individual has acquired relationships with the political world that are generally similar to those of older people in his society or subculture, as well as to those he will possess through his adult life. (This is the age at which this stage is reached in Western or Westernized nations. It is probable that this stage of development is reached even earlier in more traditional societies, in which adult status is acquired earlier.) For most individuals the core of the political self is well established before the individual becomes an adult socially.

The exact genesis of the political self is difficult to identify.

[5] The discussion in this section draws heavily upon two studies of the development of political orientations among American elementary school children. One study by Fred Greenstein was based on a sample of New Haven children in grades 4 through 8. For a comprehensive report of this study, see Fred Greenstein, *Children and Politics* (New Haven: Yale University Press, 1965). The other was based on a national sample of school children in grades 2 through 8. For reports and analysis of this study, see David Easton and Robert D. Hess, "The Child's Political World," *Midwest Journal of Political Science,* VI (1962), pp. 231–235; Robert D. Hess and David Easton, "The Child's Changing Image of the President," *Public Opinion Quarterly,* XXIV (1960), pp. 632–644; and Robert D. Hess and Judith V. Torney, *The Development of Political Attitudes in Children* (Chicago: Aldine Publishing Co., 1967).

[6] We employ the words "childhood" and "adolescence" loosely here to refer to two preadult periods. As we use the terms, "childhood" refers to the period running roughly from birth to about age 12 or 13. "Adolescence" begins at about age 13 and continues up to about age 18. These age estimates are approximate. We expect the ages to vary somewhat from culture to culture.

It begins to take form during the first few years — in Western societies, before formal schooling begins. On the basis of a study of American elementary school children, Easton and Hess say: "Every piece of evidence indicates that *the child's political world begins to take shape well before he even enters elementary school* and that it undergoes the most rapid change during these years." [7] Among the very earliest aspects of political learning is an attachment to the political community.[8] This basic orientation appears to be acquired by age five or six. This attachment to the political community and its symbols is initially emotional. It is without much cognitive or informational content. Easton and Hess liken these earliest orientations to religious feelings.[9] The child first develops an emotional identification with his nation, his tribe, or some other basic political unit.

Studies in the United States have found also that the orientations developed early are indiscriminately positive. Political leaders and symbols are regarded almost unanimously in friendly ways. The child tends to ascribe benevolent attributes and functions to the president and to other authority figures. The policeman, the mayor, and the president are visualized as providing help and services in a benevolent manner. Children in the early elementary school years see political authorities in a highly personal way.[10] Greenstein notes the following types of responses from elementary school children to questions about what the mayor, the president, and other political leaders do:

The President deals with foreign countries and takes care of the U.S. (Eighth grade boy)

The mayor helps people to live in safety. . . . The President

---

[7] Easton and Hess, *op. cit.*, pp. 237–238.

[8] We use the term "political community" in roughly the same way as Easton and Hess in *ibid.*, p. 233. They identify it as the most basic level of the political system and define it as "a group of persons who seek to solve their problems in common through a shared political structure."

[9] *Ibid.*, p. 238.

[10] See Fred I. Greenstein, "The Benevolent Leader: Children's Images of Political Authority," *American Political Science Review*, LIV (1960), pp. 934–945.

is doing a very good job of making people be safe. (Fourth grade girl)

The President gives us freedom. (Eighth grade girl)

The Board of Aldermen gives us needs so we could live well. (Fourth grade girl)

The mayor pays working people like banks. (Fifth grade boy)

The mayor sees that schools have what they need and stores and other places too. (Fifth grade girl)

The mayor helps everyone to have nice homes and jobs. (Fourth grade boy) [11]

In addition to these basic orientations toward the political community, its symbols and representatives, other fundamental attachments that significantly affect the structure and development of the political self begin during the preschool years. In American society, children identify with a political party at this initial stage. In both the New Haven and the Easton and Hess studies it was found that the majority of elementary school children were able to assert a party identification by the earliest school years investigated.[12] (Grade four for Greenstein and grade two for Easton and Hess.) Like attachments to the political community and political authorities, the initial political party identification lacks informational content. The youngest children could articulate little more than a simple identification: "I am a Democrat." Or "I am a Republican." The earliest orientation is in the form of a vague, nondiscriminating identification. Of the early acquisition of party identity, Greenstein writes:

> Here, as in children's assessments of the importance of political roles, we find that political feelings, evaluations and attachments form well before the child learns the relevant supporting information. It is not until the fifth grade that the modal child can name at least one party leader, and not until the eighth grade that the children typically name leaders in both parties.[13]

Issue and ideological orientations associated with parties do not appear until the middle or late teens. We do not have

[11] Greenstein, *Children and Politics*, p. 39.
[12] *Ibid.*, p. 21; and Easton and Hess, *op. cit.*, p. 245.
[13] Greenstein, *loc. cit.*

comparable evidence on the types of political attachments which begin at this stage in other societies, but we surmise that similar basic identifications occur at about the same time. They may be directed toward political groupings other than parties, however. For the African child, tribal identification may be roughly analogous to party identification for the American child.

In a similar manner the child acquires attachments to and identifications with social and economic classes, ethnic and racial groupings, and other significant societal categories.[14] Racial awareness, for example, appears to develop in the preschool years. Preschoolers have been found to respond to questions of racial awareness, "in a manner which indicated not only awareness of racial differences, but also the use of stereotyped roles." [15] Like other types of initial social and political learning, the child has almost no information about the objects of these attachments. They are vague self-definitions which tie him in with some people and differentiate him from others. The child knows that there are blacks and whites, Jews and Catholics; and that he is black or white, Jew or Catholic.

The early basic political learning, then, occurs side-by-side with other significant social learning. As the child begins to become aware of the political world, he simultaneously forms awarenesses of other societal groupings and definitions of his self in relation to them. He learns that he is rich or poor, one of a special elite group or of an oppressed minority group, at the same time as he learns that he is of a particular nationality or tribe and of one political party or another. These subgroup identities are important because through them the individual

14 See M. E. Goodman, *Race Awareness in Young Children* (Reading, Mass.: Addison-Wesley, 1952); E. L. Hartley, M. Rosenbaum, and S. Schwartz, "Children's Perception of Ethnic Group Membership," *Journal of Psychology*, XXVI (1948), pp. 387–398; and their "Children's Use of Ethnic Frames of Reference," *Journal of Psychology* (1948), pp. 367–386; Hess and Torney, *op. cit.*, pp. 126–172; and E. L. Horowitz, "Development of Attitudes Toward Negroes," in G. E. Swanson, T. M. Newcomb, and E. L. Hartley (eds.), *Readings in Social Psychology* (New York: Holt, 1952), pp. 491–501.

15 Harold W. Stevenson and Edward C. Stewart, "A Developmental Study of Racial Awareness in Young Children," *Child Development*, XXIX (1958), p. 407.

interprets and relates to the political world. In this manner these group identities form part of the core of the political self. The simultaneous development of these two forms of social identification — with the political community, its symbols and organizations, and with societal groupings — in early childhood help explain how subgroup orientations become part of the basic political self and why they persist as reference points for political views.

This tendency for emotional attachments to subgroups to overlap nascent political awareness is one factor that makes for explosive political conflict in the adult political world. Children learn, early and fervently, that there are significant political groupings in society and that some groups are their friends and others their enemies. The intensity of regional, racial, class, ethnic, and tribal political conflicts are attributable, in part, to these aspects of early socialization. Political friends and enemies are formed long before the child fully understands what interest or policy differences actually divide them, and may persist long after such interests or policies actually make any difference.

Between the ages of seven and thirteen the child comes to perceive and understand more abstract political symbols. For younger children political perceptions involve only highly personal and immediate symbols. By around age ten or eleven the child develops the ability to respond to more impersonal symbols. The nation, for example, ceases to be embodied by the president and begins to take on more abstract substance and differentiation. Political authorities are seen increasingly less as purely benevolent and personal and rather as possessing attributes more commensurate with their differentiated roles. The younger child can do little more than identify political leaders as good and benevolent. Older children show a capacity to go much further in identifying and explaining the behavior of political leaders and institutions. One student of political socialization, examining ten- to fourteen-year-old boys, reports an important accomplishment for the boys in early adolescence. The boys were asked why the president is reasonable most of the time. They responded that unreasonable behavior would be punished; "we would not re-elect him, Congress would not pass his bills, he would not be voted money to run the government, he might even be impeached." These adolescents indicate a more sensitive understanding of the restraints within which the president operates.[16]

Along with a growing capacity to differentiate and handle impersonal symbols and institutions, the transition from seven to thirteen years of age shows a marked increase in political information and knowledge. The increase in political information exhibited by one group of grammar school children is displayed in Table IV.1. Children in the lower grades almost universally know the name of the president and mayor, but few know much about political roles and duties. By grades seven and eight the number of children able to provide knowledgeable answers about political roles increases substantially.

TABLE IV.1   *"Reasonably Accurate" Responses to Selected Political Information Items: Arranged by School Year*[a]

| Information asked | School grade | | | | |
	4th	*5th*	*6th*	*7th*	*8th*
President's name	96%	97%	90%	99%	100%
Mayor's name	90	97	89	99	97
President's duties	23	33	44	65	66
Mayor's duties	35	42	50	66	67
Governor's duties	8	12	23	36	43
Role of state legislature	5	5	9	24	37
Number of cases	111	118	115	135	180

Interpretation: The higher the grade the more accurate the knowledge. These data show a remarkably consistent and steady development of political knowledge during the five-grade span, emphasizing again the amount of political learning that takes place during the preadolescent years.

Source: Fred I. Greenstein, "The Benevolent Leader: Children's Images of Political Authority," *American Political Science Review* LIV (1960), p. 937.

During later childhood, children's ideas evolve from nearly complete ignorance of the geographical, social, and political world around them to an outlook that is not fundamentally

[16] Roberta Sigel, "Political Socialization: Some Reflections on Current Approaches and Conceptualizations," unpublished paper presented at the Meetings of the American Political Science Association, New York, September, 1966, p. 8.

different from perceptions of mature adults.[17] Investigating
children of eleven to eighteen years, Adelson and O'Neil trace
five changes in the development of political ideas:

1. The decline of authoritarianism.
2. An increasing grasp of the nature and needs of the community.
3. The absorption of knowledge and consensus.
4. The growth of cognitive capacities.
5. The birth of ideology.[18]

They find that the most significant developments take place
between eleven and thirteen.

By the early teens, the child seems to have acquired the
major components of a mature political self. Basic political
attachments and identifications have been well established.
The strong emotional feelings regarding political institutions,
symbols, and authorities have been supplemented with knowledge of more specific roles and functions. By this time much of
the political world has been mapped out by the maturing
citizen. The remainder of adolescence is characterized by a
gradual and steady increase in political participation and involvement. The individual increasingly follows, and develops
a sense of involvement with, events in the political world.
His relationship with the political world, his political self-
identification, is crystallized as he takes on adult political
roles. Studies of the political outlooks of teenagers consistently
demonstrate that the teen years show increased frequencies of
political interest, following political events, identification
with political parties, and participation in political groups.[19]

[17] For additional research on this development, see Gustav Jahoda,
"The Development of Children's Ideas About Country and Nationality,
Part I: The Conceptual Framework," *British Journal of Educational
Psychology*, XXXIII (1963), pp. 47–60; and "The Development of Children's Ideas About Country and Nationality, Part II: National Symbols
and Themes," *British Journal of Educational Psychology*, XXXIII (1963),
pp. 143–153.

[18] Joseph Adelson and Robert P. O'Neil, "Growth of Political Ideas in
Adolescence: The Sense of Community," *Journal of Personality and Social
Psychology*, IV (1966), pp. 304–305.

[19] See Herbert H. Hyman, *Political Socialization* (New York: The Free
Press, 1959), pp. 51–68, for a review and analysis of this literature.

Ideological thinking develops and identifications with societal subgroupings increasingly take on political relevance.

Important aspects of political maturation take place during later adolescence, but most often, development during this period crystallizes and internalizes patterns established during the preadolescent period. By the end of adolescence, the political self of the average individual is pretty well established. Political maturation has been cumulative, evolving through a vague perception of the political world and emotional attachments to it, to more discrete knowledge and differentiation of political roles and objects, to a sense of active involvement in the political world.

This political maturation reflects a more general capacity of the child to think, conceptualize, and grasp abstract phenomena.[20] In their study of the growth of political ideas, Adelson and O'Neil trace the development of the sense of community along with the development of the capacity for social and political thinking from age 11 to 18 as follows:

Eleven-year-olds: "We might say that the 11-year-old has not achieved the capacity for formal operations. His thinking is concrete, ego-centric, tied to the present; he is unable to envision long-range social consequences; he cannot comfortably reason from premises; he has not attained hypothetico-deductive modes of analysis."

Thirteen-year-olds: "The 13-year-old has achieved these capacities some (much?) of the time, but is unable to display them with any consistent effectiveness."

Fifteen-year-olds: "The 15-year-old has an assured grasp of formal thought. He neither hesitates nor falters in dealing with the abstract."

Eighteen-year-olds: "Taking our data as a whole we usually find only moderate differences between 15 and 18. . . . The 18-year-old is, in other words, the 15-year-old, only more so. He knows more; he speaks from a more extended apperceptive

20 See J. Piaget and A. M. Weil, "The Development in Children of the Idea of the Homeland and of Relations with Other Countries," *International Social Science Bulletin*, III (1951), pp. 561–578; Wallace E. Lambert and Otto Klineberg, *Children's Views of Foreign Peoples* (New York: Appleton-Century-Crofts, 1966); and other work of Piaget for analysis of the development of cognitive processes in children.

mass; he is more facile; he can elaborate his ideas more fluently. Above all, he is more philosophical, more ideological in his perspective on the political order." [21]

This developmental learning pattern fits the maturation process outlined above. The most extensive increase in political learning and in the ability to think and grasp abstractions takes place between ages eleven and thirteen.[22]

ADULT POLITICAL LEARNING

Although in some respects the most important developments in the political self occur in childhood, the acquisition of political orientations — sometimes even major changes in basic loyalties and identifications — take place throughout adult life. Political learning rarely can be accomplished fully during the preadult years. Few societies provide childhood socialization experiences that fully prepare a child for the variety of contacts and experiences he will have subsequently in the adult world, though some societies obviously do the job better than others. Postadolescent socialization consequently is very important. Arnold Rose makes this point in discussing what he calls "incomplete socialization." [23] His major proposition is that children, especially in modern industrial societies, cannot be socialized sufficiently during childhood to enable them to cope with all they encounter later as adults. He points out that:

> . . . there are some special reasons in our kind of society why a significant proportion of people should grow up, perhaps get a very adequate formal education, and still not learn all of the things that are generally expected to be characteristic of a fully participating adult in a society. This we shall call "incomplete socialization" and explain the major reasons why it occurs in our type of society.[24]

Though Rose stresses the high frequency of incomplete so-

[21] Adelson and O'Neil, *op. cit.*, pp. 305–306.

[22] This age notion is supported by the Greenstein and Hess and Torney data, as well as by those of Adelson and O'Neil.

[23] Arnold M. Rose, "Incomplete Socialization," *Sociology and Social Research* XLIV (1960), pp. 244–250.

[24] *Ibid.*, p. 244.

cialization in modern industrialized societies, the same phenomenon occurs even in simple cultures.

Rose lists four major reasons why it is difficult to prepare new offspring for adult positions.[25] First, the rapidity of technological and social change makes it impossible to anticipate what the world will be like even twenty-five years in the future. The roles and behavior expected of the individual during his adult years are apt to be different from what even the most perceptive socializers anticipated and prepared him for during his childhood. Second, the world has become more pluralistic and varied, posing more and harder choices for individuals. Parochial socializing agents cannot fully comprehend and anticipate the variety of experiences and roles with which the individual may come in contact as an adult. Third, both geographical and vertical social mobility are increasingly frequent. A child socialized in a particular geographical location or social stratum may live in quite a different environment as an adult. Fourth, those responsible for training the child are fewer, more specialized, and more restricted in their knowledge of the world.

These limitations are particularly applicable to the more specialized processes of political socialization. They are relevant to both the age factor we are discussing here and the issue of continuity, which is the subject of Chapter VI. Extensive changes occur in the political world. Most explicitly political roles are reserved for adulthood. Childhood socializing agents (*e.g.*, the family and primary groups) are nonpolitical and not likely to devote much explicit attention to political training. It is thus particularly likely that childhood socialization will not do a complete job of preparing one for adult political life.

Numerous factors initiate changes in political outlook during adulthood. As an adult, the individual becomes involved in new social groups and roles which lead to alterations in his political orientations. Moving from one part of the country to another, shifting up (or down) the social and economic ladder, becoming a parent, finding or losing a job, getting old, are

25 *Ibid.*, p. 245.

common experiences that can result in modified political perspectives. Changes in the political world also make people revise
their political outlooks. Political leaders come and go. The
fortunes of political factions rise and fall. Old policy supports
disappear and new policy demands come into being. Changes
in the political world exert pressure on citizens to bring their
views into line with new conditions. The rapid and substantial
changes taking place in the developing nations today are exaggerated cases of such pressures. In these situations adult
citizens frequently are confronted with greatly altered or even
entirely new political units, for which childhood socialization
lessons have little relevance. Without the continuation of political learning during adulthood many adults would remain
incompletely or inappropriately oriented toward their political environment.

Research and information on adult political socialization
is even more sparse and less systematic than on childhood
and youth. We have no data that trace systematically the development of political orientations through adulthood. Some
research, however, indicates some general developments in
political man during adulthood. Studies from several different
nations report that the rate of political participation rises during early adulthood.[26] Substantial increases in the frequency
of voting and in identification with a political party occur
during the twenties and thirties. The frequencies reach a peak
and level off at some time during the forties and fifties, and
decline after sixty. The Michigan Survey Research Center
studies of the American electorate illustrate this general pattern in voting frequency.[27] (See Table IV.2.) Only 52 per cent
of the 21-year-olds in the 1952 and 1956 samples of citizens
reported having cast presidential ballots. By age 30 the proportion voting has risen to 70, and by age 50 to 79. A peak turnout of 82 per cent was reached at age 63, and by age 65 a steady
and sharp decrease in voting turnout began. Notice that the

[26] For an inventory of findings on this age pattern, see Lester W. Milbrath, *Political Participation: How and Why Do People Get Involved in
Politics?* (Chicago: Rand McNally, 1965), pp. 134–135.

[27] Angus Campbell, Philip E. Converse, Warren E. Miller, and Donald
E. Stokes, *The American Voter* (New York: Wiley, 1960), pp. 493–498.

greatest increase occurs between 21 and 30. Studies in other nations have found a similar development with age. Valen and Katz, interpreting this growth in party identification among Norwegian voters, comment:

> The critical point for strong identifications seems to be reached by age 30. The average Norwegian is more concerned with interests of a personal character as a young man and then becomes involved in political affairs as he takes on the roles of taxpayer, parent, and community member.[28]

TABLE IV.2

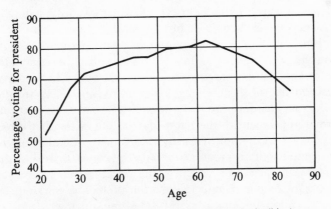

Source: from Figure 17-1, "Relation of Age to Voting Participation," in Angus Campbell, Warren E. Miller, and Donald E. Stokes, *The American Voter* (New York: John Wiley & Sons, Inc., 1960), p. 494.

The common form and substance of adult political learning is not the same across-the-board increase in basic political commitments, identifications, information, and conceptualization that characterize preadult political maturation. Normally it entails alterations such as changes in the amount and direction of political participation (*e.g.*, taking an active part in

[28] Henry Valen and Daniel Katz, *Political Parties in Norway* (Oslo: Universitets-Forlaget, 1964), pp. 211–212.

elections or not and supporting one political party instead of the other) and in the evaluation of programs and leaders. Referring back to the political maturation scheme discussed in Chapter II, it is largely the third type of political orientations which are acquired and altered during adulthood. These orientations are responses to and evaluations of specific political leaders, policies, and events. The adult may alter his opinions toward government welfare policies and develop evaluations of new national roles in world affairs, but he is not likely to alter national or group loyalties, his conception of the legitimate means of selecting political rulers, or broad ideological goals.

These distinctions are important if we are to understand what happens to the political self during adulthood. New orientations are acquired, but in most instances they occur within bounds established by the deep and persistent orientations acquired during childhood. The adult citizen may alter his opinion toward government education policy as his party's position on the issue changes, but he is not likely to alter his basic identification with a political party. In fact, the strong attachment to the party may be the factor that directs his change of opinion. He may change his evaluation of governmental welfare programs because he comes to realize that such programs are of benefit to the working class with whom he has a strong and enduring identification. The working class identification remains constant. The opinion toward governmental policy changes as the individual's interpretation of what is in the best interest of the working class changes. The basic orientations learned early also restrict the formation of new adult opinions. The adult citizen may not be able to criticize his nation's actions in the international arena because he has a strong, positive emotional attachment to his nation.

Sometimes, even basic attachments and identifications are altered in adulthood. Major political events, significant policy alterations, new political parties, new political institutions, are basic transformations in political life that exert pressure for changes or adjustments in political thinking and evaluation. The Civil War in the 1860's and the Great Depression in the 1930's led to large changes in American political orientations.[29] Party preferences are among the most persistently held and significant reference points for Americans. The Civil War and the Great Depression were the only times in which significant numbers of Americans made rapid shifts in party identification. These episodes also led to changes in the political meaning of regional identities and in expectations toward government functions. The achievement of national independence for African and Asian nations in the two decades following World War II, surrender for Germany and Japan in 1945, political and social revolutions in the Soviet Union, Mexico, Cuba, China, and Eastern Europe, likewise have called for basic and widespread adjustments in the political outlooks of the adult citizenry. The African tribesman has had to learn to live with new national governments. The conservative Catholic Pole has had to adjust to a Polish socialist regime.

Most adult political learning results from less cataclysmic events. Changes in political orientations more generally result from individual and family experiences. Experiences in work and social groups, social and geographic mobility, and participation in politics are the most common and significant adult experiences that affect political outlooks. Job experiences are one common adult phenomenon that may contribute to political learning. Seeking to understand the effect of experiences in nonpolitical situations upon political orientations, Almond and Verba asked a sample of citizens in each of five nations the extent to which they were free to participate in and to protest decisions about their jobs. They raised this theoretical issue:

> Do democratic political orientations (which include the attitude that one can be a participant in political decisions) depend upon opportunities to participate in nonpolitical social relationships? Of crucial significance here are the opportunities to participate in decisions at one's place of work. The structure of authority at the work place is probably the most significant —

29 Campbell, *et al., op. cit.,* pp. 151–153.

and salient — structure of that kind with which the average man finds himself a daily contact.[30]

In each of the five nations, individuals who were consulted about decisions on the job and who felt free to protest job decisions tended to have higher levels of political efficacy. The job participants felt that they could have some influence in the world of politics. This form of job participation is probably one of the factors leading the adults to more political efficacy. Participation in other types of social groups likewise influence adult political skills, attitudes, and values.

Changes in income level, occupation, and social and ethnic identifications often are accompanied by adjustments in political outlook. These changes expose the individual adult to new social experiences, reference groups, and socializing agents. New neighbors, work associates, and social peer groups which accompany changes in social and economic and occupational status may alter political orientations learned in childhood and youth. The boy growing up in a lower-class Polish area of a large city is likely to acquire a Polish-American identification, a self-definition as lower-class, an attachment to the Democratic Party, and accept the Catholic Church as an important reference group. These identifications are passed on and mutually reinforced by parents, relatives, neighbors, and schoolmates. If he becomes a lawyer, moves into a middle- or upper-class suburb, and joins the Presbyterian Church in adulthood, the chances are he will alter many of his political preferences. Middle-class surburbia and the Presbyterian Church may replace Polish-American Catholicism as his most important reference points. His new neighbors and work associates may replace his immigrant parents and schoolmates as norm-giving primary associates. He may switch his party preference to the Republican Party. Social mobility, with its associated changes in associates and reference groups, not uncommonly leads to alterations in political outlooks of adults.

Geographic mobility has similar results. Among the most significant type is migration from rural to urban areas. Like

[30] Gabriel Almond and Sidney Verba, *The Civic Culture* (Princeton: Princeton University Press, 1963), p. 363.

occupational and social mobility, movement from a rural to urban environment exposes an individual to new socializing experiences. An observer of the Italian political culture makes this point:

> . . . urbanization will make the individual less parochial; less tied to traditional institutions such as the family, church, neighborhood, and village; more prone to affiliate with secondary associations that provide additional political socialization; potentially, at least, more open in his political partisanship and less aloof from or hostile toward political institutions.[31]

The peasant who moves as a young man to an industrial center is likely to experience alterations in the traditional political outlooks nurtured in a rural childhood.

Adult political socialization also occurs as participation and involvement in politics develop and alter political characteristics.[32] Voting, following campaigns and policy discussions, attending political meetings, paying attention to political communications in the media, etc., can alter old and establish new political attitudes and values. By paying attention to happenings in the world of politics, one acquires new knowledge and revises old information about politics. An individual who has never voted, participated in a political meeting, talked with public officials, may find that his perceptions of the political world are altered substantially as a consequence of doing one of these. An increase or decrease in political efficacy may result from voting or petitioning public officials, depending upon the outcome of the act. Trust or distrust of these officials can be learned from experiences with political authorities. The man who is mistreated by the police, or whose petition to a public bureaucrat is arbitrarily disregarded, learns to mistrust political officials.

It is difficult to pin down exactly what types of political learning result from political participation and involvement.

[31] Joseph LaPalombara, "Italy: Fragmentation, Isolation, Alienation," in Lucian W. Pye and Sidney Verba (eds.), *Political Culture and Political Development* (Princeton: Princeton University Press, 1965), p. 325.

[32] The notion that participation in politics is important for the training and education of citizens was set forth in Tocqueville's study of American culture. See Tocqueville, *loc. cit.*

We suggest that a good deal of one's political prejudices, evaluations, and information are developed and altered in this manner. Political experience is probably one of the most important forms of political learning for many adults. It is affected, of course, by an initial predisposition toward political involvement. The individual who has never learned to be attentive to political happenings and is not brought into direct relationship with the political world is not likely to be greatly affected by experiences in politics or political happenings. This form of political learning is particularly important for the minority who are drawn into political activity and leadership.

CONSEQUENCES OF AGE AND
DEVELOPMENTAL PATTERNS

The age and developmental patterns of political learning now should be fairly clear. Political socialization begins early in life, before formal education is under way and before the child has the capacity actually to understand and order for himself abstract political symbols and relationships. Its earliest manifestations are vague attachments and identifications toward his nation, tribe, or state, important political symbols and goals, and social groups. Lacking informational content, the earliest political learning is highly emotional, much like religious feelings. For the most part the identifications and attachments acquired early are intensely and persistently held. They serve as salient categories and reference points that underlie interpretations and relationships with political events, ideas, and objects the individual encounters later in life. They are the least susceptible to change of the several types of political orientation. Orientations that are acquired later involve more information and are directed toward less basic political objects. They build upon the foundation of the basic orientations.

In late childhood the initial attachments and vague perceptions are filled in with more concrete and discriminating information. The institutions, roles, and relationships of the political world are mapped out. More explicit self-definitions and relationships with the political world are taken on. The individual has a fairly complete identity by the mid-teens, one that continues to grow and change, but whose core characteristics are firmly planted.

The early acquisition of fundamental political loyalties and their persistence through life as reference and orienting points are important for the political culture and the political system. These conditions contribute both to the stability of those systems with orderly and persisting political forms and to the lack of stability often found in new nations and in nations experiencing change. In stable polities, the strength and durability of basic orientations such as national identification, patriotism, and attachments to rules, ways of doing things, and ideologies provide a firm and stable underpinning for the fundamental forms and goals of the government. They make for continuity and intergenerational agreement in the political culture. Governments and political leaders can gauge and predict citizen reactions and expectations. If such basic attachments were acquired only late in life and were more capricious, it would be more difficult to establish and maintain a stable political culture and orderly political procedures.

By the same token, the early acquisition and tenacity of these basic orientations are a source of instability in new and changing polities. The creation of new nations, radical changes in existing ones, and attempts to integrate new groups into ongoing polities generally call forth changes in basic attachments and identities among adult citizens. The resistance of such basic attachments to change makes it difficult for adult orientations to be brought in line with altered political arrangements. Cases of this type of tension are common in the contemporary world. Most of the new nations in Africa and Asia are beset with the difficulties of reorienting adult citizens. Those societies which are trying to bring more of their citizens into political participation and national awareness often are frustrated by the persistence of previously acquired negative, indifferent, or hostile orientations concerning participation in the national system. Effective, widespread alterations in basic loyalties and identifications can take place only over several generations. In the meantime polities must operate with considerable incongruity between citizen identities and existing political forms.

The most extreme instances of extensive incongruity wrought by the persistence of childhood outlooks are found in the new nations in Africa. Many of the adults in these new polities maintain the basic political attachments to tribal and other parochial political units which they acquired during childhood before the new nation-states came into being. The persistence of these orientations has made it difficult to establish new allegiances and primary identifications with the new nations. The new nations consequently cannot count on the primary loyalties of large segments of their citizenry or widespread acceptance and understanding of their political forms.[33]

Our interpretation of the capacity for change and adjustment of adult political man remains ambivalent. Some forms of political orientations are susceptible to alteration and development during later life. Adjustments to lesser changes in the political world and one's position in it occur regularly and easily. Adult political man is capable of making some adjustments in political values and attitudes, as his own social relationships or the political world itself change. If these changes were not possible, there could be little personal adjustment and satisfaction in the world of politics. Orderly and stable political processes would be next to impossible. On the other hand, most individuals develop a core of political loyalties and attachments which are generally resistant to change in later life. They are altered only as a result of severe pressure.

[33] This notion is discussed by Robert A. LeVine in, "Political Socialization and Culture Change," in Clifford Geertz (ed.), *Old Societies and New States* (New York: The Free Press, 1963), pp. 280–303.

CHAPTER V

Methods of Political Learning

PEOPLE LEARN about politics in a variety of ways. Political learning occurs through direct teaching or indoctrination, through imitation, observation, and identification, and as a result of experiences in the political world, among the many possibilities. In this chapter we shall outline and discuss basic learning processes important in political socialization. Our major effort will be to identify and distinguish among several types of learning.

The nascent literature on political socialization identifies two very general processes through which political characteristics are acquired and developed. *Indirect* forms of political socialization entail the acquisition of predispositions which are not in themselves political, but which subsequently influence the development of the political self. Nonpolitical orientations are acquired and later directed toward specifically political objects to form political orientations. The formulation of this learning pattern is in the development of attitudes toward authority. Its major tenets are as follows: the child, as a result of his relationships with parents, teachers, and other nonpolitical authorities, develops certain expectations from persons in authority. He acquires a general disposition toward authority; not particular authorities, but authority in general. Later this predisposition is directed toward more particular political authorities; it is said to be transformed into a political orientation. If parents are permissive, political leaders come to be regarded as permissive. If parents are rigid and doctrinaire, the same qualities are expected of authorities in the political world. Indirect political learning involves two steps, acquiring a general predisposition and transferring it to political objects. This abbreviated statement greatly simplifies the notion, but it indicates the dynamics of indirect political socialization.

The phrase "*direct* political socialization" refers to processes in which the content of transmitted or developed orientations is specifically political. Whereas indirect political socialization entails the type of two-step process outlined above, this mode involves the direct transmission of political outlooks. The individual learns explicitly about the structure of his government, the virtues of a political party, or the superiority of a particular political ideology. The orientation acquired is directed toward a political object without intermediary general predispositions.

The indirect and direct learning notions should not be confused with distinctions between intentional and unintentional teaching. There is a temptation to pair indirect with unintentional socialization, and direct with intentional transmission. Such pairing is erroneous and impairs the utility of both distinctions. Direct political socialization may be intentional and overt, as when the schoolteacher urges her charges to be good citizens and to abide by the laws. Or it may entail unintentional transmission, as when the child acquires a fear of the police by overhearing older peers recount how they were chased or beaten by a policeman. Indirect socialization may be intentional, as when the child is told that the "good boy" is one who always obeys what adults tell him; or unintentional, as when the child learns the necessity of rules by participating in neighborhood sports. The critical distinction between the two modes of learning is not the overt intent of the socialization agent, but the degree to which the socialization experience is infused with specific political content.

Students of political socialization have given the two forms of political learning more or less emphasis. Some have held that the most important political learning takes place through the direct transmission of political expectations. Others have argued that less direct acquisition and subsequent transference is the more common and significant form of political learning. Of course, most scholars recognize that the two modes of political learning should not be viewed as mutually exclusive. Political maturation involves both indirect and direct forms of learning. One mode of learning may dominate one stage of political maturation, and the second mode other stages. We intend not to argue for one emphasis over the other, but to spell out the different elements of each, and to relate them to the overall process of political socialization.

INDIRECT FORMS OF POLITICAL SOCIALIZATION

Many early discussions of political socialization stressed the indirect mode of learning. Scholars pointed to the transference of those predispositions acquired in nonpolitical situations to political objects. This emphasis stemmed largely from the influence of the culture-personality or psychocultural anthropologists, from whom many of the early notions of political socialization were borrowed.[1]

The psychocultural theorists attempted to explain culture by analyzing the configuration of personality types which composed it. In explaining the development of these personality traits they focused on the cultural context and socialization experiences which gave rise to them. In keeping with their Freudian orientation, their major emphasis in explaining socialization was the experiences of the very young child within his family. Ethnographers frequently found close fits between the cultural patterns (or personality traits) of adult societies and the types of child-rearing practices employed.[2] The basic structure of individual personality presumably is formed during the first few years. Most subsequent development is determined by the dispositions established then. Explicit political orientations and other types of specific social attitudes and

[1] For an examination of this influence on the notion of political socialization see Gabriel Almond and Sidney Verba, *The Civic Culture* (Princeton: Princeton University Press, 1963), pp. 323–330.

[2] See, for example, John W. M. Whiting and Irwin L. Child, *Child Training and Personality* (New Haven: Yale University Press, 1953).

values are viewed as projections or generalizations from the personality traits acquired early in life. These notions were brought into the study of political learning as scholars attempted to explain the development of both individual political orientations and the collective political culture.

A good example of how such ideas influenced early discussions of political socialization is suggested in a 1959 statement by Almond. Pointing out the differences between indirect and direct political learning, he suggested that the most important political socialization experiences occur through an indirect process. He stressed the important role of early family experiences in shaping general personality traits and interpreted political orientations as projections from these traits. On the influence of these early family experiences he wrote:

> More of an impact occurs here than at any other point in the process. But the way in which the family citizenship analogy affects adult citizenship is quite complex and rarely, if ever, takes the form of a direct repetition of early childhood patterns.[3]

In a further elaboration of the psychocultural emphasis in political socialization analysis, Almond and Verba wrote:

> The early psychocultural approach to the subject regarded political socialization as a rather simple process. Three assumptions were usually made: (1) the significant socialization experiences that will affect later political behavior take place quite early in life; (2) these experiences are not manifestly political experiences, but they have latent political consequences — that is, they are neither intended to have political effects nor are these effects recognized, and (3) the direction of socialization is a unidirectional one: the more "basic" family experiences have a significant impact upon the secondary structures but are not in turn affected by them.[4]

The authors argue that the psychocultural approach unduly

[3] Gabriel A. Almond, "A Functional Approach to Comparative Politics," in Almond and James S. Coleman (eds.), *The Politics of the Developing Areas* (Princeton: Princeton University Press, 1960), p. 28.

[4] Almond and Verba, *op. cit.*, p. 323.

simplifies political socialization; this approach, they point out, does not explain the range of political characteristics which go into making the political self.

We share this judgment. These statements indicate the meaning and significance early students of political socialization saw in this form of indirect learning. The idea of indirect political learning is broader than the specific structure outlined by Almond and Verba, as they go on to point out. Indirect political socialization includes the following three more specific methods of learning: (1) "interpersonal transference," (2) "apprenticeship," and (3) "generalization."

1. *Interpersonal Transference.* One common form of indirect political learning has been identified by Hess and Torney as "interpersonal transference." They outline the assumptions of this form as follows:

> This model assumes that the child approaches explicit political socialization already possessing a fund of experience in interpersonal relationships and gratifications. By virtue of his experience as a child in the family and as a pupil in the school, he has developed multifaceted relationships with figures of authority. In subsequent relationships with figures of authority, he will establish modes of interaction which are similar to those he has experienced with persons in his early life.[5]

Of the three forms of indirect political socialization, this is closest to the psychocultural heritage discussed above. The notions have been applied almost exclusively to the development of authority orientations. The issue of whether the adult has "democratic" or "authoritarian" predispositions is presumed to be rooted in his earliest contact with nonpolitical authorities. In its more familiar expressions the major proposition is something like this.

If the family is authoritarian (dominated by a harsh, discipline-prone father who gives the children little chance for decision-making participation), the child will learn submissiveness and acquiescence in the face of authority. He acquires a general predisposition of submissiveness. As an adult, he comes

5 Robert D. Hess and Judith V. Torney, *The Development of Political Attitudes in Children* (Chicago: Aldine Publishing Co., 1967), p. 20.

to define his political role as one of deference to authorities over him, and possible dominance over those he considers below him. Conversely, democratic or participant family experiences (a family in which the parents share power and decision making and are more permissive in controlling the behavior of their children) are presumed to lay the foundation for democratic political orientations. The child learns to participate in decision making and not to submit blindly to persons in authority.

In addition to this focus on authoritarian and democratic predispositions, analysis using interpersonal transference assumptions has been applied to another facet of orientations toward authority. Easton and Hess use it to explain how American grammar school children acquire benevolent orientations toward the president, whom the authors view as the key authority figure in American politics. American children, Easton and Hess suggest, generalize authority orientations from their immediate experiences to perceived authorities who lie beyond their knowledge and direct experiences. As the child becomes aware of the political world and authority figures in it, he transfers his earlier nonpolitical authority experiences onto figures in the political system.

> The authority figures with which they have earliest and most
> intimate contact are of course their parents, and it is this image
> of authority that they subsequently seem to transfer to political
> figures that cross their vision. The child not only learns to respect and admire political authorities, but with regard to many
> characteristics sees them as parents writ large.[6]

Since one expects the American child to have benevolent parents, his early images of other authority figures are also benevolent. In his study of the development of authority orientations among American grammar school children, Greenstein too points out that the favorable orientations toward the president as a central authority figure may result

[6] David Easton and Robert D. Hess, "The Child's Political World," *Midwest Journal of Political Science,* VI (1962), p. 242.

from the transference of feelings toward the parents to the political world.[7]

An observer of political socialization in primitive, non-Western societies employs a similar notion of political learning. LeVine argues that orientations toward political authority result from a direct transference of family oriented attitudes to authority structures in these primitive political systems.[8] He suggests that this type of direct projection from early childhood family experiences to the political world is more likely to take place in simple societies than in complex, highly structured ones.

2. *Apprenticeship.* A second mode of indirect learning, apprenticeship,[9] is closely related to the interpersonal transference model. It differs, however, in one important respect. While the interpersonal transference form entails the direct transference of explicit predispositions which were acquired through experiences with nonpolitical role models, apprenticeship learning occurs as the behavior and experiences in nonpolitical situations provide the individual with skills and values which are used in a specifically political context. Nonpolitical activities are viewed as practice or apprenticeship for political activities. From various nonpolitical experiences the individual acquires skills and insights which he uses to find his way in the political world.

In the United States, character-training organizations such as the scouts, 4-H clubs, Little Leagues, etc., are important for this form of political learning. In such organizations a child learns to compete, but to compete only within the rules; he learns to want to win, but to accept defeat with grace; he learns to choose leaders by popular vote, and to punish their mistakes by voting them out of office. He learns, among other

[7] Fred I. Greenstein, "The Benevolent Leader: Children's Images of Political Authority," *American Political Science Review,* LIV (1960), p. 941.

[8] Robert A. LeVine, "The Internalization of Political Values in Stateless Societies," *Human Organization,* XIX (1960), pp. 51–58.

[9] As far as we know this term has not been used in the literature to refer to a form of indirect political learning. We feel, however, that the word "apprenticeship" puts across the key ideas we are referring to.

things, how to act in competitive but regulated situations. The relevance of such activities for the role of an adult citizen in a two-party democracy is obvious. In other societies, youth groups and play groups are structured in other ways and serve as apprenticeship settings for acquiring other types of skills relevant for their political arrangements. Donald N. LeVine reports in his analysis of the Ethiopian political culture that in children's groups the child learns to submit willingly to a defined authority.[10] This pattern, he reports, is consistent with relationships in the political world.

As with the first type of indirect political learning, the idea of apprenticeship learning has been applied to the analysis of participation and authority. Almond and Verba, suggesting modifications in psychocultural hypotheses, include school and work experiences as nonpolitical settings in which apprenticeship learning takes place. They retain the ideas of indirect political learning and the analogy from nonpolitical to political situations. Using the school and work setting in addition to the family, the age of indirect learning experiences is expanded to include late childhood and adolescence (school) and adulthood (work). Expanding the notion of indirect political socialization to include training for political roles or what we have identified as apprenticeship, they point out that:

> . . . the role that an individual plays within the family, the school, or the job may be considered training for the performance of political roles. . . . Participation in non-political decision making may give one the skills needed to engage in political participation: the skills of self-expression and a sense of effective political tactics.[11]

Two important aspects of indirect political socialization hypotheses are suggested here. First, indirect political socialization is not arrested in childhood but continues throughout life. Second, indirect political learning is not restricted to transference of expectations from nonpolitical role models to political persons. It includes also the acquisition of skills,

[10] Donald N. Levine, "Ethiopia: Identity, Authority, and Realism," in Lucian W. Pye and Sidney Verba (eds.), *Political Culture and Political Development* (Princeton: Princeton University Press, 1965), pp. 250–251.
[11] Almond and Verba, *op. cit.*, pp. 327–328.

habits, behaviors, and practices appropriate for political activities.

The data collected by Almond and Verba in the five-nation study support these contentions. Participatory experiences in the family, school, and job are all related to the quality of participation in political life. They also find that the effect of participation in the making of decisions in these three settings is cumulative. The individual who has consistent opportunities for participation in each of the three nonpolitical areas is more likely to generalize the effects of such participation to the political world than the individual who participated in one nonpolitical area but not in others.[12] Participating in the nonpolitical decision making in later life tends to offset the lack of such opportunities in childhood. Family experiences are neither the only nor necessarily the most significant experiences that help prepare individuals for participation in the political world.

The transfer relationship may proceed in both directions. Democratic norms and opportunities for participation in the political world may generate pressure for democratic arrangements and the right to participate in nonpolitical situations, as well as the other way around. The effectiveness of the political order in setting norms, and of political experiences as training or conditioning for other types of social relationships, should not be overlooked. The political world can serve as a model for other organizations. The stress upon membership participation and democratic forms in secondary organizations, schools, and even work groups has been influenced greatly by the democratic norms of the political world. Contemporary American college students pressuring for increased student participation in the making of university policies are taking democratic values and rights from the political world and arguing that they should be followed within the university. Since we live in a democracy and presume to follow democratic procedures as a nation, university decisions should be made according to democratic procedures. This is a major aspect of the rationale of students demanding more "student power." In developing nations, demands for popular partici-

12 *Ibid.*, p. 366.

pation in political life are followed by demands for popular participation in labor unions, schools, and even the family. If it can be assumed that the sharing of decision-making authority in the family can help maintain the democratic state, it is also likely that the democratic state helps to maintain the participant family.

3. *Generalization.* This variation of indirect political socialization is closely related to the two major forms already reviewed. In many instances political attitudes developed as social values are extended toward specifically political objects. An individual's general belief system has latent political content. Verba writes persuasively on this point:

> The basic belief and value patterns of a culture — those general values that have no reference to specific political objects — usually play a major role in the structuring of political culture. Such basic belief dimensions as the view of man's relation to nature, as time perspective, as the view of human nature and of the proper way to orient toward one's fellow man, as well as orientations toward activity and activism in general would be clearly interdependent with specifically political attitudes.[13]

The logic of this proposition can be demonstrated by several examples. In Mexico a general feeling of ineffectiveness seems to find political expression as an attitude of political alienation. Italians are distrustful of their fellow man; they also approach politics and politicians with a good deal of cynicism. Uneducated Africans frequently look upon natural calamities like drought with fatalistic resignation. They regard government in the same way. The common man can no more control the centers of political power than he can manipulate the centers of naturalistic powers.

The relationship suggested in these cases is important. A person's political self is embedded in his entire belief system. The process by which he acquires the belief system, then, contains latent consequences for his political maturation. We cannot begin to review the rich and complex process by which the belief system is acquired. But generalizing from general social values to political objects is one important means by

[13] Sidney Verba, "Comparative Political Culture," in *Political Culture and Political Development, op. cit.,* pp. 521–522.

which the political self is developed. It is one form of political learning.

This brief outline of indirect political socialization suggests several generalizations. First, the initial emphasis of the psychocultural approach on child-rearing practices is unduly restrictive. Such an approach either fails to explain adequately, or does not allow for, important political socialization which takes place later in life. Rigid adherence to the psychocultural hypothesis would require that one interpret all post-childhood socialization as projections or extrapolations from the basic personality traits developed in early childhood. Second, indirect socialization encompasses types of learning other than the transference from role-models which has been its major focus. We have suggested two additional forms: apprenticeship and generalization. Third, empirical work using indirect political socialization models has focused on a narrow range of political orientations: those directed toward authority relationships and participation. Of course, it may be that these are the political orientations for which indirect learning is most important. Indirect political socialization is unlikely to be as significant for, say, acquiring a sense of national patriotism, party identification, or issue positions. To explain the entire spectrum of political learning it is necessary to consider also direct forms of political socialization.

DIRECT FORMS

The second general category under which we can distinguish modes of political socialization is the notion of direct learning. This idea refers to experiences in which learning is explicitly political. Just as we identified several variations of indirect political socialization, we can suggest several forms of direct political learning: (1) imitation, (2) anticipatory political socialization, (3) political education, and (4) political experiences.

1. *Imitation.* This is the most extensive and persistent mode of social learning known to man.[14] Young and old, the intelli-

14 For a discussion of the role of imitation in social learning, see Miller and Dollard, *Social Learning and Imitation* (New Haven: Yale University Press, 1941).

gent and those less so, depend on imitative learning. It is applicable to a wide array of values, behaviors, skills, expectations, and attitudes. The importance of imitation in social learning is illustrated by watching a child learn to talk and walk. The most basic skills the individual acquires, communication and mobility, are acquired by the child in large part by imitating what he sees and hears.[15]

Imitative learning may be a conscious, deliberate effort, or it may involve unconscious copying of values and behavioral patterns from others. Consciously or not, children pick up an important part of social, cultural, and religious preferences from adults by taking parental values and adopting them as their own.

Well over half of the children studied by Greenstein and by Easton and Hess had formed some sort of identification with a political party by age seven or eight. Since it is doubtful that many of the parents or teachers specifically taught political party identification to the children at this early age, it is likely that the children came to a party preference by copying their parents. In later years teachers, friends, spouses, and work associates, as well as more public persons and opinion leaders, become sources of political values and attitudes also by imitation. The close correspondence in political outlooks found among peers and work associates seems to indicate that imitation of some sort serves as a means of socialization within such relationships.

Aspects of social imitation are at the heart of theories of socialization and attitude acquisition, such as small group analysis, reference group theory, symbolic interaction theory, and what Smith, Brunner, and White designate as the social adjustment function of adopting and holding opinions.[16] Very generally, each of these frameworks of analysis portrays the individual as imitating the attitudes of those people he is with — or would like to be with. He imitates their behavior so that they will accept him into the group. The child imitates the

[15] Frederick Elkin, *The Child and Society* (New York: Random House, 1960), Chapter 3.

[16] M. Brewster Smith, Jerome S. Bruner, and Robert W. White, *Opinions and Personality* (New York: Wiley, 1956), pp. 39–47.

party identification of his parents because they are significant persons in his life. The foreign immigrant or the rural-urban migrant imitates the political orientations of those in his new environment because he wants to be identified with and accepted by them.

The obverse of political imitation is a situation in which the child deliberately rejects the values of parents or other authorities. This is a sort of negative imitation, or what reference group theorists call a negative reference group effect.[17] It is an act of rebellion. Reverse imitation sometimes takes place among adolescents, as they seek to shape an identity which differentiates them from parents and other authorities. Under certain conditions (when politics is highly salient to both the rebel and the ones rebelled against), this process can significantly alter the political self. The classic example of such rebellion is the youth from a conservative upper- or middle-class home who joins a radical political group as an act of rebellion against his parents. The basic dynamics of rejecting the values of the imitated are similar to those taking place when the values are adopted.

2. *Anticipatory Socialization.* This mode of learning, similar to imitation, is appropriately labeled by sociologist Robert Merton.[18] People who hope for professional jobs or high social position frequently begin to take on the values and behavior associated with those roles long before they actually occupy them. This is most clearly seen in professional schools. Law students and medical students, for instance, begin to think and act like lawyers and doctors.

This type of socialization is less obvious in the analysis of political learning, but it undoubtedly occurs. Student activists often begin to prepare themselves for elective office before they are old enough to vote. In anticipation of holding a position of political power in the future, they begin to take on mannerisms and styles they consider appropriate for the politician. In some instances the role of "citizen" or "good

17 See Herbert H. Hyman, "Reflections on Reference Groups," *Public Opinion Quarterly*, XXIV (1960), pp. 383–396.

18 Robert K. Merton, *Social Theory and Social Structure* (New York: The Free Press, 1949), p. 265.

citizen" may be so well defined by parents and teachers that the child or adolescent can anticipate and prepare himself for it. If good citizens are supposed to be knowledgeable about public affairs, the child may begin to read the newspaper or to study weekly news readers at school.

3. *Political Education.* This term is applied to direct, deliberate attempts to transmit political orientations. Instruction in politics is carried on by the family, the schools, political or governmental agencies, and innumerable groups and organizations. Unlike imitation and anticipatory socialization, the initiative in this form of political socialization is taken by the socializer rather than the individual being socialized.

Most societies have both formal and informal channels for the direct teaching of socially valued political attitudes and behavior. The range of techniques is immense — a propaganda rally in Nuremberg Square, an initiation ceremony among the *Masai* in East Africa, the falsification of history in Soviet textbooks, a civics course in Great Britain, the biennial "get out the vote" campaign in the United States, the morning singing of the *Marseillaise* in the French village school, the political circuses in Conakry, Guinea — are a few of the ways in which societies attempt to communicate approved political values and habits.

The importance of political education is apparent. In the first place, citizens need some minimal information about political duties and rights to operate in the political arena. Obeying laws, especially those concerned with paying taxes, military obligations, and protection of property, is critical if governments are to operate effectively. Citizens ignorant of their obligations will serve neither themselves nor the state. We thus expect that, at a minimum, a society will establish some means of educating new citizens in their political duties and responsibilities. Along with this minimal political education, most societies make available to their citizens extensive information about their government, how it works, what the accepted goals are, and so forth.

Possibly much more important, the society will have methods of political education which encourage loyalty, patriotism, and support for the political institutions. Most formal schooling includes in the curriculum a full ritual life — pledging allegiance, saluting the flag, commemorating national heroes, singing the national anthem, etc. — which is intended to bind the child affectively to his nation. Direct political education is sufficiently familiar to our readers, that it is not necessary to develop the topic at greater length. One variation of political education, however, is less obvious and merits special mention.

Political education through manipulation is probably more frequent than most of us realize. The word is used here not in a pejorative sense, but rather to suggest a particular type of political education. We often find people whose social experiences have been structured in such a way that the probability of the subject's adopting one set of political values and foregoing a competing set is greatly enhanced. This conscious structuring of politically relevant experiences can be called political education through manipulation.

Much of the debate about school integration policies in the United States is essentially about the merits of different patterns of social experiences. It was argued in the classic *Brown v. the Board of Education of Topeka* that Negro children denied the advantages of interacting with middle class white children would be socially and intellectually stunted and, consequently, less competent participants in the social, economic, and political life of the nation. Bussing Negro students into white neighborhood schools is justified as an effort to guarantee that Negro and white alike will develop sociopolitical values free of stereotypes generated by isolation. The logic of this argument for political socialization is obvious: social experiences — in this case, racial segregation and isolation — condition sociopolitical values — in this instance racial stereotyping and prejudice. By rearranging social experiences — creating interracial exposure and contact — new political values, presumably more appropriate ones, will be adopted. The mode of learning implicit in this notion is simply that which results from exposure to new situations. The student is exposed to a political learning situation which would have been denied him if social experiences had not been manipulated.

The literature on nation building is full of similar examples. Political leaders are self-consciously attempting to shape political values by structuring the social experiences of the citizens, or citizens-to-be. The school system in particular is viewed as a vehicle for this type of political education. An example from East Africa is the problem of primary school dropouts (finishing primary school but not continuing to the secondary schools), who leave the farms and migrate to urban areas, hoping to find white-collar work; the problem has grown acute. A strategy adopted in some schools to counter this tendency has been to include some work on an experimental farm as part of the curriculum. The aim of the schools is to show the student that farming need not be the dull, marginal work which many students feel it is. It is shown rather as both exciting and productive. The political orientation of the student (the urge to swell the ranks of the urban unemployed rather than work on a farm is seen as a political orientation in the East African context) is affected by the deliberate structuring of his school experiences so that he will be exposed to new ideas about farming.

4. *Political Experiences.* A final type of direct political socialization results from political experiences. As we have suggested, some of what an individual learns about politics comes from his interactions with political personalities, structures, and events. Though many important political socialization experiences take place in pre- and extrapolitical settings, we should not forget that much of what a person comes to believe and know about politics follows from his observations of and experiences in the political process. The classic formulation of this notion is found in the work of Tocqueville. Traveling through early nineteenth-century America and watching the young republic struggle with the issues of democracy, liberty, and equality, Tocqueville observed that participation in making political decisions in itself produces a sense of political responsibility. When a man feels he can participate in directing his social and political destiny he is more likely to adopt a pragmatic approach to politics. He learns to compromise, to accept when he must even policies that are counter to his own wishes.

Tocqueville's writings are but one of many in the literature of political analysis which point out that observation of and involvement in the political process can substantially shape political orientations. Another relevant notion is that the tendency to support political arrangements is affected by the degree to which persons are satisfied with the activities or outputs of the government. David Easton has built a major theory of political life around the notion that nations attempt to gain their citizens' support by producing public policies which will both satisfy current citizen demands and anticipate, hence regulate, future demands.[19]

Another example of political socialization through political experiences is the way in which people come to feel politically self-confident — to feel they can influence political action. The many studies of political efficacy have demonstrated that the most advantaged members of society tend to have a stronger feeling of personal competence about politics than do less advantaged members. Nonpolitical social experiences are generalized to include the political sphere. However, the studies do not stop here. It has also been discovered that one's political self-confidence is nurtured by situations in which the government is responsive. This basic attitude of political efficacy is influenced as much by "success" in the political sphere — measured by the degree to which wishes are transformed into realities by the political process — as it is by success in nonpolitical spheres of life.

Political socialization, then, can result from direct contact with political processes, a contact not directly mediated by any political socialization agency. This kind of political learning is more frequent among adults than among children. It is only as an adult citizen that one has the opportunity for frequent and intimate contact with government officials and policies. On the other hand, children can and do have some specific political experiences which can condition their way of viewing the political world. A prime example is experiences with the police. The slum child develops from his experiences a picture of the policeman, and perhaps consequently of political authority in general, which is quite different from that of the

19 David Easton, *Systems Analysis of Political Life* (New York: Wiley, 1965).

suburban middle class child. To the slum child the policeman is a symbol of force, punishment, and at times, brutality. To the middle class child the policeman is a benevolent figure who helps elderly ladies across the street and rescues cats from the neighborhood trees.

Epilogue. We have reviewed three types of indirect and four types of direct political socialization. These various modes of socialization suggest the complexity of the processes through which individuals acquire their political selves. Any individual is likely to learn about the political world in all these ways. We have tried, where feasible, to suggest what types of learning experiences are most closely related to particular stages in political maturation and to particular types of political orientations.

It is difficult to examine in any systematic way the mechanisms through which persons acquire their political views. It is easier to study what views citizens have — the dependent variable in political socialization — or what agencies influence their views — the independent variable. It is not nearly so easy to examine the learning process intervening between socialization agent and acquired values. Subsequent chapters reflect this fact.

Many of the political socialization studies we review throughout this book are attitude surveys, conducted particularly among school children. This research is useful for telling us what people believe about politics at different stages in their life cycle. But it is not always possible to move from attitude survey data to an understanding of how people come to hold their beliefs. A major gap in political socialization theory, then, concerns the actual learning mechanism. As one critic has put it, political socialization ". . . is a misnomer for what we study because we study *what* children have learnt . . . not *how* they have learnt it." [20] We have identified some possible areas of research; we have not mentioned many specific research projects because at this stage of scholarship, little else is possible.

[20] Roberta Sigel, "Political Socialization: Some Reflections on Current Approaches and Conceptualizations," paper presented to the American Political Science Association, New York, September, 1966, p. 3.

CHAPTER VI

Discontinuities

THE PREVALENCE OF DISCONTINUITY [1]

The pacing of political maturation and the methods through which political learning takes place are but two of the factors characterizing the process of political socialization. We now turn to a different, though related, question. To what extent is political socialization characterized by discontinuities? By "discontinuity" we mean conditions in which socialization agencies and experiences do not correctly anticipate the attitudes and behavior associated with adult political positions and do not prepare the maturing individual for them, as well as situations in which an individual learns one type of political values from some agencies of socialization and different values from other agents. We say that political socialization has continuity when the early socialization experiences effectively transmit information, norms, and attitudes appropriate for political life. The obverse, discontinuous political learning, occurs when orientations acquired are not congruent with the realities of political life.

Two distinguishable patterns are implicit in this notion of discontinuity. These two forms may be identified as "congruence" and "consistency." On the one hand, discontinuity

[1] In working through the notions of continuity and discontinuity in political socialization the authors have been influenced by Sidney Verba's "Comparative Political Socialization," paper prepared for the Sixtieth Meeting of the American Political Science Association, Chicago, September, 1964.

involves a lack of congruence or "fit" between the political perceptions and values an individual has and the realities and requirements of the political world. In many instances the two are not congruent. On the other hand, discontinuity entails a lack of consistency in the messages passed on by different agents of political learning. We discuss these forms of discontinuity in the paragraphs that follow, distinguishing between the issues of congruence and consistency. In the remainder of the text, however, we will deal with the two patterns together, using the common term "discontinuity."

Discontinuities involving a lack of congruity between orientations and political realities occur when political orientations acquired during one period (childhood, for example) are not congruent with the characteristics and expectations of political roles during another (adulthood). The child may learn correct information about the political world during childhood, but by the time he reaches adulthood that world may be substantially altered. The orientations learned so well during childhood may not be appropriate for the new political forms. German children reared during the 1930's and early 1940's were taught to be strongly nationalistic and militaristic, to believe in the superiority and special destiny of the German nation, and to support a particular authoritarian leadership. The same generation of Germans, grown to adulthood in the 1950's, are confronted with a different Germany; at least officially, ultranationalistic and militaristic sentiments are discouraged and democratic political values are encouraged. In this case political lessons learned early are not appropriate for later political requirements. An adult generation may pass on its political norms to members of the younger generation quite thoroughly; but the adult generation may itself be out of tune with the political life styles called for.

This conception of discontinuity in social learning or cultural conditioning was first formulated by the anthropologist Ruth Benedict in the 1930's.[2] She approached the issue as discrepancies between what a child is taught during his formative stages and the type of knowledge and values he is expected

2 Ruth Benedict, "Continuities and Discontinuities in Cultural Conditioning," *Psychiatry*, I (1938), pp. 161–167.

to have as an adult. Childhood socialization, she pointed out, is rarely designed to prepare the individual for the roles he is faced with when he reaches adulthood. In many societies there are substantial differences between the values and behavior taught to children and the types of orientations expected of them as adults. In some cultures children are carefully sheltered from unpleasant aspects of life. When they become adults, they are expected to face life realistically, to comprehend the bad as well as the good. Discontinuity or incongruity such as this creates problems in adjustment that affect both the individual and the society. Many adults are not prepared for their adult roles. They have to learn or unlearn social orientations late in life or face some type of maladjustment.

Incongruities of this form are common in all societies. They are most acute and exaggerated in societies undergoing rapid change. Even in more stabilized, older nations, however, incongruities are rarely eliminated completely. It is in the nature of political socialization to anticipate the future imperfectly. Youths being inducted into a political culture are insulated in part from the realities of the political world which they will face as adults. Information about politics taught to the maturing citizen in the schools and other agencies of political learning rarely presents a fully accurate picture of the complexities of the world of politics. Even in nations like the United States and Britain, which have stable political practices, much experience in transmitting political norms, and extensive and subtle socialization mechanisms, youthful political idealism often is shattered by the "realities" of the adult political world. No transmission mechanisms, however comprehensive and inclusive, can fully close the gap between youthful anticipation and the real political world.

The second form of discontinuities, inconsistency in the political lessons taught by different agents, is no less frequent. The family, in talking about politics, may stress the corrupt nature of politics, the untrustworthiness of political leaders, the ineffectiveness of government. At the same time the political lessons in the school curriculum may emphasize the great wisdom of statesmen, the moral goodness of political heroes, and the successes of government programs. What is taught in one arena is not consistent with what is taught in another. Inconsistencies may occur when different agents simultaneously transmit contrary political viewpoints and when a socialization agent operating now passes on orientations different from those passed on by another at an earlier time.

Such inconsistencies are frequent in political learning. They are more or less extensive in all societies. As with the other form of discontinuity, however, they are most acute in changing societies. In the contemporary world they are especially so in societies moving from traditional to modern political arrangements and styles.[3] In transitional societies different socialization agents with conflicting political outlooks compete for the loyalty of the young. One agent maintains and transmits political values and habits associated with the traditional way of life; others emphasize values and loyalties associated with a modern or modernizing polity.

A youth growing up in a rural village in one of many transitional countries of the contemporary world very early learns important lessons about politics and authority relationships. The young must defer to the old. Leadership in social, religious, and political affairs is achieved through seniority. Hierarchies are established according to traditions which are not to be questioned. The youth learns patience and tolerance in the face of authority exercised by elders in keeping with traditional forms. Now let us assume that this boy does well in primary school, passes his examinations in secondary school, and goes to the nation's major university in the capital of his country. In this new setting he is exposed to different socializing stimuli. He learns that positions of authority should be achieved by talent and accomplishment. He finds that egalitarian notions are in vogue, and that age in itself does not connote greater wisdom, nor constitute an automatic basis for authority. Moreover, he learns that he can and should do something to alter the traditional order of things. We need not explore all the ramifications of this example to see that his return to the home village will be marked by friction. The

3 See, for example, Robert A. LeVine, "Political Socialization and Culture Change," in Clifford Geertz (ed.), *Old Societies and New States* (New York: The Free Press, 1963).

family and village leaders will resist his new ideas and urge him to return to the traditional ways. The youth has been exposed to incongruent socialization agents and experiences: there has been considerable discontinuity in his political learning.

If we multiply this experience, and allow for minor variations, we have a picture of conflict between generations which is common in much of the world today. Experiences of this kind are frequent in the new nations of Africa and Asia, in much of Latin America and Eastern Europe, and to a lesser extent even in the more highly industrial nations of the West.

As with other aspects of political socialization, the issue of discontinuities has both an individual and a systemic component. At the individual level, it affects the fit between the political self developed as a result of one stage of socialization and the demands of the polity. Or it influences the congruence between the content of socialization messages emanating from different agents. Are the orientations toward political authority developed during the important childhood years congruent with the realities and demands of the adult political world? Do the family, schools, peers, and adult social groups present the individual with similar or differing cues regarding political life?

At the system level the key question is whether the political culture matches the structures and processes of the polity. Are the orientations making up a particular political culture congruent with the forms and operation of the polity? Is the system able to create or maintain a political culture consonant with its basic institutions and processes? If a system has democratic institutions do its citizens accept, support, and value democratic processes? If it has a socialist regime does the political culture include a preponderance of orientations regarding socialism as a proper political form? Discussions of the political culture and the political system generally assume a close relationship between the subjective distribution of orientations toward political actions and the actual properties of the polity. This notion is implicit in our discussion of political culture in Chapter III. One of the major values of studying the political culture and political socialization pat-

terns is that political orientations affect the form and operation of the polity and vice versa. In some instances, however,
the discrepancies between a polity and its political culture can
be very great. In periods of rapid political and social change
such discrepancies may be both extensive and long-lived. The
issue of the level of congruence between structure and culture — between the actual properties of a system and subjective orientations toward it — is complex. How much incongruity a system can endure without serious threat to its
stability is a very important question, and one which contemporary political theory has not dealt with adequately.[4]

Discontinuities are quite common in political socialization.
There is a great likelihood that all the agencies of political
learning with which the individual has contact will not transmit the same political lessons, and that political forms and
processes will not always match the individual's political
education.

CAUSES OF DISCONTINUITY

We have hinted at some causes of discontinuities in political
learning; we shall now outline these sources more systematically. The major proposition presented thus far is that political learning is likely to include some discontinuity. Four
major characteristics of political learning contribute to this.

First, there is a time lag between the period when much of
the crucial political learning takes place and the time the
individual takes on explicitly political roles. Though much
political learning takes place during childhood and early adolescence, explicitly political roles — voting, petitioning public
officials, paying taxes, belonging to social and political organizations — are assumed during adulthood. Political learning of
school children seems to take place before or during the junior
high school years, yet legal access to many citizen roles is not
granted until age 21. Proponents of lowering the voting age
in the United States to 18 point out that the lower age level
would be closer to the time when young people finish their
secondary education, an experience presumed to involve po-

[4] David Easton discusses this issue in some detail in his *A Systems
Analysis of Political Life* (New York: Wiley, 1965), Chapters 10–15.

litical education and motivation. They argue that the individual is more likely to vote and better prepared to understand political processes when his basic education reaches its peak than after he has been out of school for two or three years. Their goal is to close the gap between the end of formal education (for most youngsters) and the assumption of political roles.

This time lag contributes to other sources of discontinuity as well. It is quite possible that the political arrangements toward which early orientations are directed will be extensively altered after early orientations are acquired and before adult political roles are assumed. Wars, invasions, uprisings, depressions bring into being new political orders for which the parental generation could not have prepared its offspring. Technological changes alter society and create new activities which political socialization agents of the immediate past had no way of anticipating. Changes in the international sphere, a new political ideology, and domestic policy changes may alter the political world within a few years, and prevent any parent generation from anticipating the political world for which it must fit its youth.

A third source of discontinuity, also related to the time lag, lies in the various agencies and experiences that help in developing the political self. The family, schools, peer groups, adult occupational groups, political parties, and governmental actions all influence the dissemination of political orientations. These agents cannot be expected always to hold and transmit identical political information and values. Different agents attempt to push the individual in different directions. The child in an ethnic ghetto of an American city may acquire a Democratic Party identification and positive orientations toward the welfare state. As he grows up, goes to college, takes a management job in a bank, and moves to the middle class suburbs, he is exposed to different socializing agents. These are not likely to hold and transmit the same political norms he received from family and neighbors in the ghetto.

A fourth source of discontinuity (or error) is the discrepancy between the close, personal relationships of family and friends in which early political learning takes place and the

impersonal, highly structured situations of adult political behavior. The early experiences are not always appropriate for
establishing successful orientations toward the secondary structures of the political world. This source of discontinuity is
particularly likely to occur in states with more formal political
relationships.

These several sources of discontinuity in political learning
occur in all societies. In most countries the overall process of
political socialization is likely to be characterized by some
discontinuity. As Verba says of the sources of discontinuities,
". . . Somewhat paradoxically, the most potent socialization
experiences are located at a far remove from the political system. The wide distance between primary socialization agencies
and the political process suggests further that political socialization is a process with many discontinuities in it." [5]

SYSTEMIC SOURCES OF DISCONTINUITY

The amount of discontinuity in political learning is not the
same in every polity. The process is likely to be more discontinuous in some types of polities than in others. As a very
general outline we suggest that the following systemic conditions are related to the level of discontinuity: (1) the complexity and heterogeneity or level of devlopment of the polity;
(2) the range of agents performing political socialization; (3)
the amount of geographic and social mobility in the society;
and (4) the amount of change or stability experienced by the
society.

1. *Societal Complexity and Heterogeneity.* Discontinuity is
likely to be more common in complex societies — those with
differentiated political roles and institutions and heterogeneous cultures — than in simple societies which lack specialized
political structures. Among other factors, cultural heterogeneity and specialized political institutions lead to a greater
gap between primary socializing institutions, such as the
family and peer groups, and the more formal secondary political relationships. Some of the crucial conditions affecting
discontinuity in political maturation stem from the differences
inherent in early socializing experiences and in the political

5 Sidney Verba, *op. cit.,* p. 2.

world. Differences in both time of impact and in nature of relationships are important. Since the family universally is a major source of political learning, the discontinuity depends, in part, upon the correspondence between its socialization effect, that of other agents, and the style and substance of relationships in the world of politics.

Close and direct fits between primary group experiences and those in politics are most likely to occur in primitive, simple societies. Robert A. LeVine points out that in simple, "stateless" societies the type of authority system found in the family is generalized fairly easily to the somewhat unspecified political system.[6] The child acquires attitudes toward authority in the family that are generalized later to the political structures. In simple societies there is often a direct and congruent relationship between the family authority system and that of the polity. The polity is, so to speak, the family on a large scale. This form of continuity and direct generalization are less likely to occur in more complex systems; at least the relationship is not so direct. Cultural homogeneity contributes to generalization of family authority patterns onto the polity. Cultural heterogeneity, on the other hand, hinders this process. LeVine offers several hypotheses outlining conditions that affect the congruence between family authority and authority relationships in the political world:

1. The degree of congruence is inversely related to the amount of social stratification.

2. The degree of congruence is inversely related to the specialization and stability of supra-community political structures.

3. Among societies of a given level of political integration (such as the local community or nation), the degree of congruence is directly related to the presence of corporate descent groups, the degree of localization of descent groups, and the use of kinship terms within territorial units.

4. Among societies of a given level of political integration, the degree of congruence is inversely related to the presence of procedures for secondary socialization such as schools, institu-

6 Robert A. LeVine, "The Role of the Family in Authority Systems: A Cross-Cultural Application of Stimulus-Generalization Theory," *Behavioral Science*, V (1960), p. 295.

tionalized peer groups, and military training programs, through which actors in the political system must pass.[7]

In complex societies, political life is more different from family life than it is in simpler societies. Family life is characterized by dependence of the children on the parents. Social and biological differences between adult and child necessitate some sort of hierarchic arrangement in which the parent cares for and controls the offspring. Highly personal, face-to-face relationships characterize family life. In contrast, political life in the complex society is not usually characterized by as great a dependency relationship. The citizen does not stand in the same relationship to government as does the child to the parent. Political authority is rarely accepted in the way authority in the family is. Political authority is contingent on the continued support of the population. Further, political life is characterized by impersonal, secondary relationships rather than personal, primary ones. The average citizen knows his government only through the large and impersonal bureaucracy which administers the programs and policies of public authorities. Whereas family roles are diffuse, political roles are functionally specific. In the family, the role is never separated from the incumbent. Quite the opposite is true in political life. Citizens recognize the permanence of a role regardless of the incumbent. "The King is dead, long live the King!"

For these and similar reasons, the social and political experiences in family life are not always transferable to relationships in politics. The attitudes and skills needed for effective political operation can be learned only partially in the family. The more differentiated the polity, the less effective the family.

Since the effect of the family is limited, agencies other than the family are important in political training in complex societies. Eisenstadt suggests that, in complex industrial societies, age-homogeneous groups (groups with members of comparable age and status, and thus unlike the family) are needed to supplement the socialization experiences of the family.[8] These groups are structurally more congruent with adult social and

[7] *Ibid.,* p. 295.

[8] S. N. Eisenstadt, *From Generation to Generation* (New York: The Free Press, 1956), especially Chapter 2.

political relationships. Where the family and other early primary relationships do not adequately equip the individual for participation in the political world, socialization experiences with other agents are necessary. The formal educational system is probably the most common and significant institution performing such a function. The political cues, values, predispositions, and skills acquired in the schools are often at odds with those picked up from life in the family; but at the same time they may be more appropriate for political life. In this sense, discontinuities between socializing agents are necessary for both the individual and the nation. If the family does not successfully socialize its offspring into the polity — and we have suggested a number of reasons why it often cannot — some discontinuities in political socialization experiences are necessary and desirable. The discontinuities may involve adjustment tensions for the individual, but in time the result will be beneficial.

2. *Number and Variety of Socializing Agents.* Discontinuities in political learning are more likely to occur when a number of different agents participate in political socialization. The number and diversity of agents engaged are related to the development and complexity of the political and social systems. This statement may seem tautological but it helps clarify the point. More highly developed and complex societies are likely to have a variety of agents engaged in political socialization. In simple societies the family is often the only significant socializing institution; at the other end of the scale — in highly developed nations such as the United States, Britain, West Germany, the Soviet Union — numerous agencies instruct politically. Specified educational institutions, occupational and civic associations, ethnic and religious organizations, mass media, and governmental agencies perform the socialization task along with the family.

All agents do not always pass on the same political cues. Attitudes toward partisanship fostered by school experiences are likely to differ from those learned in the family. Norms concerning political participation and minority rights advocated by government agencies may not resemble those stressed by regional, religious, or ethnic groups. In European nations, socialist oriented labor unions may teach the individual worker attitudes and hopes proper to his role in the political world which differ from dispositions he acquires in a lower class or peasant Catholic home and Catholic schools. In developing societies an activist, mass political party passes on to the peasantry political expectations different from those acquired in the traditional tribal family and village.

This source of discontinuity is prevalent in heterogeneous societies, even those characterized as stable. In societies with multiple socialization structures there is rarely total continuity in the socialization cues emanating from the various agencies. The amount of noncongruence, and its implications for both the individual and the polity, however, varies even among complex societies. In diversified political cultures, like those of France and Italy, the differences between the political orientations taught by a conservative Catholic family, the governmental school system, a socialist oriented labor union, and proletarian parties are great. It is not uncommon for individuals in these nations to have contact with each of these types of socializing agents.

In other instances a multiplicity of socializing agents does not seem to cause extreme discontinuities. In the United States, discontinuities between political learning in family, school, youth groups, occupational organizations, and governmental agencies appear to be relatively slight. Nonauthoritarian values, national loyalty, and democratic commitments are shared by nearly all socialization structures. We do not mean that there is full congruence among socializing agents, but rather that the discrepancies are relatively slight. Donald N. LeVine reports a high level of congruence in political learning within different socialization agents in Ethiopia, a nation not as developed as the United States but with a number of socializing agents.[9] A common orientation toward authority prevails in the family, play groups, the schools, adult associations, and relationships with the emperor and other political authorities. This orientation entails, basically, obedi-

[9] Donald N. Levine, "Ethiopia: Identity, Authority, and Realism," in Lucian W. Pye and Sidney Verba (eds.), *Political Culture and Political Development* (Princeton: Princeton University Press, 1965), pp. 245–281.

ence to authority without question, and expecting services from those in authority. The genesis of this orientation is in the family where obedience is the prime socialization objective:

> This experience in the family is continuous and consistent with the rest of Amhara culture. Children and adolescents acquire a disposition to respect and obey authority which is generalized to all other spheres of their life. Even in children's play groups there is a pronounced tendency to define someone — usually the eldest — as an authority figure and to submit willingly to his ideas and impulses.[10]

3. *Social and Geographic Mobility.* Population mobility also contributes significantly to the discontinuity in political learning. Societies within which people move from place to place, and up and down the socioeconomic ladder, are likely to have more political socialization discontinuities than those with static populations. The more movement there is within the society the more likely people are to be exposed to different agents of social learning and to different political norms and attitudes. Much of the social and political meaning of mobility stems from the resulting exposures to new agents of political socialization. Movement from rural to urban areas, migration from one geographic or political region to another, change from one population subgroup to another, and movement from one social or economic stratum to another may create discontinuities in political maturation. The rural dweller who moves to an industrial city, the provincial peasant who migrates to the metropolitan center, and the lower class boy who enters a high status occupation, are confronted with political pressures and cues in these new positions that are not congruent with previous experiences.

Migration from rural to urban areas is one of the most socially significant phenomena in developing and industrializing societies. In nearly all nations of the contemporary world, large numbers of people are moving from agricultural localities to commercial and industrial urban centers. In many instances this migration means movement from a tradi-

---

[10] *Ibid.*, pp. 250–251.

tional environment to a more "modern" one and entails significant changes in economic, social, and political experiences. Such migration means exposure to new and different social and political structures which result in significant discontinuities in political learning. In this type of movement the amount of socialization discontinuity, political and otherwise, depends on the extent of the differences between rural and metropolitan environments, as well as the extent to which the nation has a homogeneous political culture extending through all parts of the society.

Migration from a traditional peasant area in northeastern or southeastern Poland to metropolitan Warsaw involves more discontinuity than migration from rural areas in central Ohio, Indiana, or Illinois to Chicago, Detroit, or Cleveland. Rural Poland is more different from urban Warsaw than is rural Ohio from Cleveland. Common orientations concerning political life are more evenly distributed throughout American society than in Polish society. Rural and urban dissimilarities are even more pronounced between the "bush" areas of Kenya and Uganda and large cities such as Nairobi and Kampala. Rural to urban migration in these cases can cause extremely great discontinuity. Discontinuities resulting from rural-urban migration are likely to be greatest in the developing areas and new nations.

Moving from one economic or social position to another involves contact with new and different political socialization structures, and consequently with different orientations toward the political world. Because variations in political outlook and socialization agents with varying political orientations are distributed according to social and economic levels, the individual who moves from one position to another is likely to experience some political socialization influences which are not congruent with his previous political learning. The peasant son who becomes a worker in a steel mill, and the "poor boy" who makes good as a doctor are likely to find pressure for changes in political orientations among the consequences of changes in position. The extent of discontinuity accompanying this type of movement depends upon the divergence of political outlook between occupants of different strata. In some societies, changes in social position bring great pressures for radical changes in orientation toward the structure and nature of the political universe. In others, upward social mobility is likely to involve little more than pressure for change in political party identification and attitudes toward some types of governmental activity.

4. *Political Change.* A final condition determining the level of discontinuity in political learning is change in the structure and processes of government itself. Of all sources of discontinuity, those resulting from political change are potentially the most disruptive for a nation as a whole for individual adjustment. Political forms are dynamic rather than static. The contemporary social and political world is characterized by widespread and extensive change. Not only are established political systems moving through more or less significant transformations, but many new states have been brought into existence. Though we know little about the causes and processes of political and social change, current knowledge does suggest that significant gaps, or time lags, can exist between political structures and their respective political cultures. Political structures and institutions change more rapidly than the constituent orientations toward them. The structure and operation (if not its effectiveness and stability) of the political life of the Congo have preceded the development of national identification with and loyalty to the Congo as a political community. In the Soviet Union the political system came into existence prior to the Sovietization of the Russian people. The Soviet Union early acknowledged this situation and attempted to remedy it. Since the Revolution in 1917 the leaders of the Soviet Union, conscious of the lack of congruity between the Soviet regime and Russian political culture, have tried deliberately to alter the situation through programs of political education.[11]

Differences between the rates and substance of change in political systems and in political culture are a major source of discontinuity in the development of political orientations. The fact that the constitutional order is likely to change before the

11 See Frederick C. Barghoorn, "Soviet Russia: Orthodoxy and Adaptiveness," in Pye and Verba, *op. cit.,* pp. 450–511.

96

Processes

political culture means that polities experiencing change will have population elements whose orientations are not congruent with existing political arrangements.

The source of many of these discontinuities is inherent in political socialization. Individuals acquire basic political orientations — especially those toward the boundaries, structure, and operating procedures of the political system — at a very early age. These orientations tend to persist throughout the life span. Thus, many constituents within a nation have fundamental political orientations that were developed a generation or more earlier. Political changes are not reflected rapidly in, or followed immediately by, related alterations in constituent orientations, since many adult citizens persist in orientations acquired during childhood socialization experiences. This point is borne out by studies of voting behavior and political attitude showing that older citizens have political orientations somewhat more similar to the political culture of a previous period.[12] In the United States, older voters are more likely than younger voters to be Republicans and to be opposed to welfare state principles, orientations more prevalent when they were growing up than in the contemporary period.

The level of discontinuity resulting from political change very much depends on the extent and rapidity of that change. Political instability is present in some newly independent African nations because they have not yet developed a citizenry with strong national identities and loyalties. This proposition is developed and analyzed by Robert LeVine, who investigated the problem of socializing the constituents of the new nations in Africa and Asia, bringing them into loyalty for and identification with their new national political systems — i.e., the problem of nation building.[13] Building from the studies of childhood socialization in American society, he points out that one of the main problems in these new nations is that adult constituents were socialized as children into political allegiances, loyalties, and identifications directed

[12] See Angus Campbell, Philip E. Converse, Warren E. Miller, and Donald E. Stokes, *The American Voter* (New York: Wiley, 1960), pp. 153–156.

[13] Robert A. LeVine (1963), *loc. cit.*

toward local and tribal units. These local units persist as the primary points of political identification for large numbers of the citizens. The new nations are forced to operate within a political culture made up of primary political loyalties and identifications directed not toward the national political community but toward local and tribal units. There is extensive discontinuity between the political orientations of the citizens and the new political order. Because of persisting political loyalties acquired in childhood, LeVine suggests that this noncongruence can be rectified only over a considerable period of time. Political instability is likely to be the rule rather than the exception in these areas for some time to come. Further, today's parents find their basic political identification in non-national political units. Inasmuch as most political socialization still occurs in the family, local rather than national identification is likely to be the major focus of primary socialization for a long time. Political change in societies with less of a gap between the extant and the needed political beliefs is less extensive and disruptive.

PART III

Agents

POLITICAL SOCIALIZATION is performed by a variety of social agents. All societies have institutions that develop and transmit political knowledge, attitudes, and values among their members. This is true of primitive polities which lack specialized structures as well as more complex systems with specialized political institutions and roles.

The agents taking part in political socialization vary from society to society. Some agents are institutions set up for the specific purpose of passing on political values or developing awareness and support of the political arrangements. Political youth groups, political parties, civic and political education courses in the schools, and government propaganda bureaus are such special agencies. Other political socialization takes place within institutions only marginally concerned with transmitting political orientations. Nonpolitical agencies often pass on political norms while engaged in other activities; the family is the prime example. Families are neither instituted nor organized specifically for transmitting political values. Yet almost universally the family serves as a major agent of political socialization. Peer groups, occupational, religious, and social organizations, and general educational institutions may be placed in this same category. These groups only occasionally are organized for political purposes, but in many instances they are significant in forming political views. Political learning is often an unintended consequence of nonpolitical relationships. Parents pass on political values to their offspring, not so much through deliberate indoctrination or teaching, as through a less intentional process of imitation or osmosis.

Political socialization occurs through both primary and secondary relationships. The distinction between these two forms of relationship is important for understanding political learning. Primary relationships are highly personalized and relatively unstructured; examples are those which take place among members of a family, close friends, and work associates. Much of an individual's time is spent in primary relationships, and they universally serve important socializing functions. Secondary relationships, on the other hand, are more formal and impersonal. As a rule secondary relationships involve a less total involvement by the individual. Political parties, labor unions, educational institutions, and mass media are secondary institutions that socialize politically.

These distinctions are important for understanding the range of experiences contributing to political learning and the relative significance of different agents of socialization. All societies have a complex mixture of primary and secondary relationships, although secondary structures are less extensive in more primitive societies. By and large, the relationship between man and his government is rarely highly personal and unstructured. This is particularly true of the more highly developed societies. One of the primary attributes of more developed states (i.e., a major factor that distinguishes them from more traditional or less well developed polities) is that they have specialized, secondary institutions for carrying out political socialization. Political organizations, civics courses, and political communications in the mass media help educate politically. These distinctions, however, are only relative. Primary relationships exist even in highly complex societies. One of the central propositions in political socialization theory is that primary relationships universally are important for the formation of political orientations. Even in the most highly developed systems — *i.e.,* those with the greatest number of specialized secondary institutions engaged in political tasks, such as the United States, Britain, the Soviet Union — primary institutions persist as potent agents of socialization.

The fact that primary relationships are major sources of political learning has important consequences for the overall form and impact of political socialization. First, the fact that political relationships are largely secondary, whereas much of socialization results from primary relationships, contributes to some forms of discontinuity in political life. Family and peer group relationships are not similar to those of political life. For this reason they cannot fully and successfully prepare an individual for participation in the secondary institutions which constitute the political world.

More significantly, this predominant role of primary agents means that political learning for a society as a whole is unorganized, decentralized, varied, and nondeliberate. The crucial role of primary groups, especially in the early, formative years of political maturation, renders it difficult for the government or any central agency to completely control or manipulate political loyalties and values. Explicitly political organizations, many secondary groups, the educational curriculum, and the mass media can be more or less effectively programmed by central leaders. Some governments have been fairly effective in controlling political parties and organizations, dictating the political policies of trade unions and business associations, specifying the content of political education in the schools, and regulating the political content of communication media. In contrast, primary groups such as the family, close friends, and work groups are largely beyond the reach of direct, centralized control. Even the most highly developed and technologically efficient governments cannot effectively oversee the political learning that takes place in these primary groups. As long as many different, uncontrollable relationships serve as sources of values and information, political socialization will not be totally programmed.

It is also significant that for most primary groups, and even for many secondary ones, contributing to political socialization is not a central group task. Only in rare instances are primary groups specifically political. The cell units associated with the Communist Party and the small, tight cadre of revolutionary or subversive political movements are exceptions of some importance. The family, friends, and work associates pass on political values, but usually not in any deliberate and systematic fashion. The socialization efforts of such groups are likely to be sporadic and incomplete.

We do not wish to imply that secondary institutions are unimportant in political socialization. On the contrary, especially in the more highly developed polities, a number of secondary institutions are influential. The school system is a widespread and important secondary institution for political learning. Occupational organizations, political groups, and the mass media are also important. Despite the development and operation of these secondary institutions, many of which attempt deliberately to influence political learning, much political socialization occurs through primary relationships.

The undirected nature of primary group socialization makes it unlikely that a nation will have an entirely homogeneous political culture. Families and primary groups will socialize differently. Both the extent to which political socialization is engaged in and the content of political lessons taught varies from group to group. One family may diligently teach its offspring the duties of a citizen and conservative political values, while another may neglect to stress citizen obligations and espouse liberal politics. Citizens are not likely to be uniformly educated about a common politics.

The major role of primary groups also imbues political socialization with a conservative bent, making it difficult for a political culture to be altered rapidly and uniformly. Nations like the Soviet Union and Communist China, which have engaged in attempts to alter fundamentally and systematically their political cultures, have experienced difficulties in this regard. The leaders of these nations have responded in part by breaking down traditional primary relationships, diminishing the power of the family and other primary ties. These efforts were initiated because the family was viewed as a protector and transmitter of traditional (nonsocialist) orientations. The nation building efforts in Africa and Asia also have been frustrated by the persistence of the family in passing down traditional political loyalties. Messages supporting changes in political information and values can be disseminated more rapidly and consistently through secondary institutions — *e.g.*, the schools, mass media, and political parties. These structures are more easily manipulated. The lingering traditional outlook of families and peer groups, coupled with their strong and lasting influence upon individuals, however, mitigate the effectiveness of such efforts by secondary institutions. Changes in political cultures are, for this reason, slow and uneven. Traditional outlooks linger on, even after they are no longer appropriate for a changed political world.

CHAPTER VII

The Family

PRIMARY GROUPS

The primary relationships most important for political socialization are those taking place in the family and in small peer groups. These two primary structures are among the most important instruments of political and social learning.

Primary groups are small, informally structured, and characterized by personal and deep emotional relationships between members. They generally involve a high degree of face-to-face contact. For group members being together with the other members is valued in itself and is the major value the group provides for its members.[1] For secondary groups, on the other hand, the major factor that brings members together and gives the group influence over its members is the creation of some sort of social product — something produced as a result of joint action. Relationships are more formal and members work together in order to achieve some other social goal. The personal relationships are not the crucial value derived from the group by members. The family, small friendship cliques, and small groups of work associates are the most common primary groups. Labor unions, political organizations, and school classrooms are secondary groups involved in political socialization.

The family is the most significant and universal of social

[1] Scott Greer, *Social Organization* (New York: Random House, 1955), p. 34.

institutions. It is the most important source of primary relationships for most people in all societies. Nonfamily primary groups, such as close friends and work associates, can be placed under the general heading of "peer groups." For our purposes it is useful to distinguish between these two types of groups. Both are characterized by primary relationships, but the way in which they are structured and their most representative relationships are significantly different. These basic distinctions are important for the way in which each of them influences political socialization. They have their major socializing effect at different ages and are influential in developing different types of orientation.

The parent-child relationship of the family is necessarily hierarchic. The family unit is composed of at least two generations. The positions of parent and child, especially during the important early stages of child development, are clearly distinguishable. The most important social purposes of the family, including the socialization of children, can be performed only under these conditions. Infants and very young children cannot be taught effectively by peers; parents and children cannot be equals in the early stages of socialization. Exaggerated and prolonged dependency of children on their parents is the most important characteristic of the human family.

Peer groups, on the other hand, are nonhierarchic primary groups, composed of members of about the same age, or who at least share equal status in their relationships with each other. Play groups in childhood, friendship cliques in youth, and small work and social groups in adulthood are the most common of these peer groups. Though these groups may have leaders, they are not made up of well defined and rigid role relationships such as those characterizing the family.

The distinction between peer groups and families is not always so clear. There are family relationships — husband-wife, siblings, etc. — that are more like peer groups than like the hierarchic family we have been talking about. In this discussion we use the word "family" only in referring to the parent and children family group. We consider more nearly equal family relationships as a type of peer group.

THE FAMILY

The family exists universally as the most significant primary institution and as an important source of social learning. Although concrete data analyzing the role of the family in all societies and a comprehensive explanation of the family as an agent of political socialization are beyond reach now, this seems an accurate and generally applicable proposition. The family affects basic political orientations very strongly. It is a key agent through which the political culture is transmitted from one generation to the next. This proposition further holds true for all political systems — those in which the family is only one of many institutions, as well as those in which it is one of a few (or the only) significant socialization agent.

The influence of the family in political socialization varies in accordance with the number and effectiveness of other socializing agencies, as well as the thoroughness with which family units perform the socialization process. Generally speaking, the family will have less overall influence when other important primary and secondary institutions take part in socialization. When family units fail to inculcate their offspring with political orientations and other institutions are available, these other institutions are likely to be proportionately more influential. The converse of this proposition is equally true. In societies without secondary institutions the family is likely to have almost a monopoly over political socialization. Even though there are these variations in relative influence, however, the family generally stands out as the most important agent determining the extent and direction of political learning. Its most serious competitor in developed nations is the school.

The prominent role of the family in the development of the political self parallels its dominant role in more general socialization — in the development of basic personality traits and other social attitudes and values.[2] This potent socializing role stems from two important factors. First, the family has access, in many instances approaching a monopoly, to the child dur-

2 Frederick Elkin, *The Child and Society: The Process of Socialization* (New York: Random House, 1960).

ing the formative years when the foundation of his political self is being developed. It is significant also that the orientations acquired in early childhood — *e.g.,* national, tribal, or community identities; perceptions of social groups; acceptance or rejection of various political structures and processes — tend to be the most intensely and persistently held of all political views. They serve as the base on which later political learning is built. In this way the influence and learning of childhood profoundly affect later political development. The family, thus, has considerable and sometimes exclusive influence on the child during some of the most critical years of social learning.[3]

The second factor is that the relationships and personal ties developed in the family are among the most important and emotionally intense the individual ever develops. Few human relationships match the strength and depth of those between parent and child, and none compete with them during the early years of childhood. How much a person is affected by others depends heavily on the depth of the emotional ties between them. This notion is the key to understanding the particular potency of the family and of other primary relationships. The more intense and emotionally involved the relationship, the more influence it is likely to have on the development of social and political behavior. It is these joint phenomena of extensive access and strong emotional ties, occurring during the formative years, that give the family such a prominent part in political socialization.

The family influences its members in political socialization in a number of ways. First, through example and direct teaching or indoctrination the family passes on political values to its offspring. Using the terminology developed in Chapter V, we may say that the family carries on various forms of direct political socialization. The deliberateness or explicitness with which this is done varies from family to family, as does the actual extent and substance of what is taught. Because parents influence their children so deeply in the early years, the political lessons a family chooses to teach are highly effective. For

[3] *Ibid.,* p. 47.

the same reason, the lessons a family fails to transmit are difficult to make up in later life.

Second, the family is important in developing a child's personality and his nonpolitical social attitudes and values. It affects nearly all forms of social learning. These personality factors and social orientations condition the acquisition of political orientations in what we referred to earlier as "indirect political socialization." Personality traits and social attitudes condition the way in which individuals respond to more specifically political phenomena.

In a related vein, the family is also the major source through which the young individual develops his own basic self-identification.[4] The self-concept is developed by relating with others. The individual first learns who he is by the way in which others with whom he has close contact (parents and fellow siblings) react to him. The first experiences of this type take place within the family. The family is the first provider of one's physical and psychological needs. The consequences of this family function have been stressed by one commentator as follows: "The family is the most prominent environmental source not only of what may be deemed its inherent function of providing affection but also of satisfying other needs. This is probably the central reason that the individual comes to think and act like his family more than he thinks and acts like those who are less regularly relevant to his need satisfactions."[5] The self, needless to say, molds the way in which the maturing individual relates to the political world. One aspect of this self-identification is specifically political, what we have called "the political self."

The family also affects political outlooks by placing its members within a network of social and economic relationships. It is primarily through the family that the individual acquires his locations in the vast social world. His ethnic, linguistic, religious, and social class, his cultural and educational values

[4] See, for example, Robert F. Winch, *Identification and Its Familial Determinants* (Indianapolis: Bobbs-Merrill, 1962).

[5] James C. Davies, "The Family's Role in Political Socialization," *The Annals of the American Academy of Political and Social Science*, CCCLXI (September 1965), p. 12.

and achievements, his occupational and economic aspirations, and his exposure to others are determined largely by his family. Like other aspects of family influence, this is particularly true for the formative years, but it often continues throughout life.

The individual's position in the social world, in turn, has a direct bearing on the content of political maturation. On the one hand, a person's social locations serve as important categories according to which the individual interprets and relates himself to the political world. In other instances they act as additional agents of socialization. Membership in or identification with a social class, a racial or linguistic group, or a religion are established primarily by the family. More often than not they serve as reference points for political attachments and interpretations, rather than as agents of political socialization. Labor unions, farmers' organizations, trade associations, on the other hand, often serve as agents of political learning, propagating some political values and attitudes among their members. Membership in these groups often is established, directly or indirectly, by the family. In this manner the family influences the development of political orientations in ways other than its own direct and indirect political socialization. By establishing their children in a particular social setting, parents help determine how they will view the political world and with what other socializing agents they will come in contact.

These factors account for the important influence of the family on political socialization. The family's role is particularly strong in forming the basic foundation of the political self, but its influence continues to shape the individual throughout his life.

THE FAMILY AND POLITICAL LEARNING

Evidence analyzing the explicit role of the family in political learning is limited and fragmentary. There is enough, however, to allow preliminary analysis, leading to tentative propositions. The most common and extensive form of evidence consists of data demonstrating correspondence in political orientations between parents and offspring.

A number of studies have investigated the association between the political attitudes and behavior of individuals and those of their parents. Overwhelmingly, these investigations have shown that individuals tend to have political attitudes and values like those of their parents. Reviewing data from perhaps 100 such studies, Herbert Hyman reports finding a very clear pattern of correspondence between parents and offspring for a wide range of politically relevant attitudes and values.[6] He reports that, on the whole, the associations are strong and that only in the area of opinions concerning war did parental-offspring opinions diverge enough to support negative correlations.

The data analyzed by Hyman are drawn exclusively from Western nations, mostly from American studies. We would expect, however, that in non-Western societies also, members of the same family tend to hold similar political views. In fact, the relationships in non-Western, more traditional societies may well be even greater. As a rule family ties are stronger in traditional cultures, and there are not as many other agents of socialization. Only in those rapidly changing societies in which conflict between generations is intense are political orientations not likely to be tied to the family context.

Hyman further reports that the correspondence between parents and offspring is particularly strong in American society for political party identification.[7] In the American polity, party identification seems to be the orientation transmitted most successfully and persistently through the family.[8] We have already remarked that the learning of party identification takes place quite early and that this identification serves as an important reference point for the citizen's conceptual organization of the political world. The fact that children have acquired a party identification by the time they are seven or eight is another significant piece of evidence suggesting that

[6] Herbert H. Hyman, *Political Socialization* (New York: The Free Press, 1959), p. 72.

[7] *Ibid.*, p. 74.

[8] See, for example, Angus Campbell, Philip E. Converse, Warren E. Miller, and Donald E. Stokes, *The American Voter* (New York: Wiley, 1960), pp. 147–148; Robert E. Lane, *Political Life* (New York: The Free Press, 1959), pp. 204–208.

basic political orientations originate in the family framework.

A closer look at some of the studies demonstrating correspondence between the political orientations of parents and
their children suggests other important facets of the family as
an agent of political socialization. When parents do not have
well developed attitudes toward politics, or have never discussed politics with their children, the children are less likely
to be interested in the political world. According to a 1952
study, American voters who came from homes in which
neither parent voted, or no parental party preferences were
made known, were less likely to develop party identifications
of their own than those who could identify their parents' party
preference. Data from this national survey are shown in Table
VII.1. Less than 1 per cent of those who could identify the
party preferences of their parents gave responses falling in
the category labeled "None, minor party, or not ascertained."
On the other hand, 22 per cent of those who did not know the
party preferences of either parent fell into this category, as
did 15 per cent of those reporting that neither parent voted.
The data are limited in scope but the implications are significant. Almost all of those coming from homes in which
there were fairly clear political party preferences acquired
a party identification, with a large majority adopting the party
of their parents. Those from homes where there were no cues
to party preferences showed two significant tendencies. First,
they were less likely to have developed any identification with
a major party. Second, when they did acquire a party identification, it was often weaker than that of individuals coming
from more partisan homes.

Though these data pertain only to political party identification, such allegiances are the central orientation in American politics, the key mechanism through which Americans
relate to their political world. In American politics a lack of
party identification usually goes with low levels of political
information and involvement.[9] Political party identification
is one of the key orientations that differentiates the more
highly politicized citizen from the apolitical one.

[9] *Ibid.*

TABLE VII.1 *Relation of Parents' Party Identification to That of Offspring*

"Do you remember when you were growing up whether your parents thought of themselves as mostly Democrats, or Republicans, or did they shift around from one party to another?"

Party identification	Both parents Democrats	Both parents Republicans	One Democrat, one Republican	One Democrat or Republican, other uncertain	Both parents shifted	Don't know about either	Neither parent voted
Strong Democrat	36%	7%	12%	14%	11%	15%	15%
Weak Democrat	36	9	32	23	23	21	22
Independent Democrat	10	6	10	13	13	14	14
Independent	3	4		10	14	5	15
Independent Republican	3	10		10	12	11	7
Weak Republican	6	30	22	12	14	9	9
Strong Republican	6	33	22	15	11	3	3
None, minor party, or not ascertained	a	1	2	3	2	22	15
Total	100%	100%	100%	100%	100%	100%	100%
Number of cases	657	387	41	102	103	140	59
Proportion of total sample a	41%	24%	3%	6%	6%	9%	4%

a Omitted from this table are 125 respondents whose parents belonged to minor parties, whose parents had unusual combinations of party connections, who did not grow up with their parents, or from whom this information was not ascertained.

Source: Angus Campbell, Gerald Gurin, and Warren E. Miller, *The Voter Decides* (New York: Harper & Row, 1954), p. 99. Reprinted by permission of Harper & Row, Publishers.

Similar parental influence on party identification has been found in other Western nations as well. A study of French political party orientations reports the same type of relationship between knowledge of paternal identification and the likelihood that a Frenchman will have a party identification of his own. In a survey of the French electorate, Converse and Dupeux found that, as in the United States, those unable to identify their father's party preference were much less likely to have a party preference of their own.[10] Knowledge of paternal party preferences was low. Only 25 per cent of the Frenchmen were able to identify a paternal political party preference. The low frequency of party identification, and the even lower frequency of ability to identify parental preferences, is, in large part, attributed to the failure of the French family to provide cues, examples, or education about political parties. We assume that these factors are related to the proposition that political party identification is not as crucial a means of identification with the political system for the French citizen as it seems to be for the American. Studies of the Swedish and Norwegian electorates suggest similar relationships.[11] Sweden and Norway fall between France and the United States in both the proportion of the electorate reporting a party identification and the frequency with which party affiliation is passed on by the parental family.

Despite these differences in the frequency of party identification and its varying role in the nation, the pattern of parental influence is the same. When political cues and examples are absent in the family, or at least not perceived by children, the children are less likely to develop them. The family is an important transmitter of political party orientations. These relationships, however, are only relative. The data in Table VII.1 also indicate that many individuals from nonpartisan homes did acquire a party identification (and, we can assume, other political orientations as well) even when parental teach-

---

[10] Philip E. Converse and Georges Dupeux, "Politicization of the Electorate in France and the United States," *Public Opinion Quarterly*, XXVI (1962), pp. 1–23.

[11] Georg Karlsson, "Political Attitudes Among Male Swedish Youth," *Acta Sociologica*, III (1958), pp. 220–241.

ing and example were absent. The family is only one of the sources of political party identification, though probably the most important. Other agents teach or transmit political orientations when the family has not done so. Other socialization experiences can substitute for, and add to, political learning (or a lack of it) in the family. It is doubtful, however, if later socialization experiences can make up completely for the absence of family socialization during early childhood.

Unfortunately, we do not have adequate data analyzing the family transmission of other types of basic political orientations. The Greenstein and the Easton and Hess studies show that children have begun to acquire feelings of national identification and loyalty and to develop views about political authorities and symbols before they begin school. Even at this early period some children have more clearly defined political orientations than others. We may assume that these differences result from varying socialization experiences in the family, but the studies do not provide enough data to permit this analysis.

There are data showing that parent-child relationships, similar to those involving party identifications, also influence the development of political interest and participation.[12] Politically involved individuals tend to be products of politically interested families.[13] Parental political interest, or a lack of it, is one of the most important factors determining whether or not an individual becomes actively involved in politics in much the same way that parental party identification seems to be an important antecedent of political party preferences. Again, there is no one-to-one relationship between parent and child in political involvement. Other socialization factors may intervene to move the individual away from parental practices and teaching toward more or less political involvement. But, despite the possibilities of other influences, the

[12] Kenneth Prewitt, "Political Socialization and Leadership Selection," *The Annals of the American Academy of Political and Social Science*, CCCLXI (September 1965), pp. 105–108.

[13] Dwaine Marvick and Charles R. Nixon, "Recruitment Contrasts in Rival Campaign Groups," Dwaine Marvick (ed.), *Political Decision-Makers* (New York: The Free Press, 1961), p. 209, and Rufus P. Browning, "Business in Politics: Motivation and Circumstances in the Rise to Power," (unpublished Ph.D. dissertation, Yale University, 1960), p. 2.

family seems to be the most crucial influence in initiating and sustaining political involvement.

We have focused primarily upon the question of whether or not the family possesses political orientations and attempts to pass them on to its offspring. The socialization influence of the family is related also to a variety of family relationships and structures.

One of the most comprehensive studies of the family's influence and that of other primary groups on political orientations is that of McClosky and Dahlgren.[14] From a study based on extensive interviews with adults in the Twin City area (Minneapolis-St. Paul), they draw the following inferences about the differential impact of the family:

1. The family is a key reference group which transmits, indoctrinates, and sustains the political loyalties of its members. Voters who support the party favored by their family develop firmer and more consistent habits of party allegiance than voters who renounce the family preference.

2. Family influence on the stability of a voter's preference increases when (a) the party outlooks of its members are homogeneous; (b) political interest and loyalty among the other members are high (this affects direction or preference more than stability, however), and (c) the same family preference has been retained over time. Family influence on party allegiance becomes strong, in addition, when its members like and often see each other; however, these factors undermine the party loyalty of voters who have rejected the family preference. The family thus serves as a continuing agency for defining party affiliations of its members. . . .[15]

These inferences contain important suggestions about the likelihood and extent of family influence upon political orientations of its members. As with many of the other data cited, the McClosky and Dahlgren study is concerned primarily with orientations toward political parties. Their analysis provides additional evidence supporting the notions dis-

[14] Herbert McClosky and Harold E. Dahlgren, "Primary Group Influence on Party Loyalty," *American Political Science Review*, LIII (1959), pp. 757–776.

[15] *Ibid.*, p. 775.

cussed above. The family's influence is related in part to its political involvement, with the more highly politicized family having a greater effect. Three important points are suggested. First, the family influence is likely to be stronger when the members' viewpoints are homogeneous. A family with varied or divided political loyalties and orientations is less effective in passing on firm and stable orientations to its new members than is a politically homogeneous one. This notion is also supported by the data presented in Table VII.1. Individuals with parents of divided party loyalty, or families in which only one parent had a party preference, are less likely to have a strong party preference than are those in which both parents identify with the same party.

A second important proposition is that the family is likely to have more influence when the family members are close to each other and when the amount of interaction between family members is great. This follows from the observation that much of the particularly strong influence of the family as a socializing agency results from the intensity of emotional bonds and attachments which generally exist between family members. Political involvement and socialization efforts on the part of the family being equal, family influence will vary according to the closeness of ties and the amount of interaction between family members. The higher the rate of interaction, and the stronger the emotional ties between child and parent, the greater the impact of the family unit on the development of political orientations.

The strength of these ties is relevant even when the child reaches adolescence and young adulthood. This assertion is supported by a study of the relationship between political positions of college students and those of their parents.[16] In a study of 1,440 college students, it was found that students who reported "not being very close," or actually "hostile," to their parents were more likely to deviate from parental political positions than were students who reported being "fairly close," or "very close" to their parents. Even among youths

16 Russell Middleton and Snell Putney, "Political Expression of Adolescent Rebellion," *American Journal of Sociology*, LXVIII (1963), pp. 527–535.

who were not so close to their parents the rate of deviation was not very great. Several explanations are possible. The parents may not have substantially influenced the children's political attitudes in the first place. The children could have been rebelling against recognized parental norms, or they may have been influenced more strongly by other socializing agents.

A further idea contained in the McClosky and Dahlgren studies is that the family influence on political orientations continues throughout life. Most notions of the family as an instrument of socialization focus on childhood learning experiences, on the influences of the parents and older members upon young children. Although this is where the most extensive and significant influence occurs, the impact of the family, and of family relationships, in later life should not be overlooked. As McClosky and Dahlgren suggest, even during adulthood family preferences influence those of participating members. In these circumstances, as suggested early in this chapter, the family in form and type of relationships operates as a peer group. The family serves as a continuing reference group, not only for the initial establishment of political orientations, but also determining their strength and stability. If an individual agrees with other family members, family relationships strengthen and stabilize his political positions. If he disagrees with most other family members, the family can weaken his deviating orientations and draw him toward the family position.

The studies reviewed here appear to contradict the popular notion of late adolescence and young adulthood as periods of rebellion against parental and family political norms. Instead of children adopting dissimilar attitudes and affiliations as a means of rebelling against parental authority, it appears that there is a particularly high level of agreement between parents and their children in party identification, voting preferences, levels of political involvement, and some other political orientations. A study of American presidential voting in 1948, for example, found that young voters were more likely than older voters to agree with their parents both in party preference and voting intentions.[17] The authors hy-

17 Bernard Berelson, Paul F. Lazarsfeld, and William N. McPhee, *Voting* (Chicago: University of Chicago Press, 1954), p. 89.

pothesize that this relationship results from the fact that younger voters have not yet been exposed to the variety of adult social groups and influences that the older voters have. As a consequence their political orientations are more firmly embedded in their family than are those of the older citizens.

Lane explored the proposition of adolescent rebellion more explicitly in depth interviews with fifteen working class and lower middle class American men.[18] On the basis of his analysis he suggests that rebellion against one's father is not particularly common in American society. He explains this, in part, by suggesting that the permissive family and the lack of father domination make such rebellion unnecessary for the process of growing up. He suggests further that even when such a rebellion does take place, the relatively low salience of politics makes other forms of rebellion more appealing than political deviation.

Three other studies, though their authors agree that adolescent rebellion in political orientation is not the prevailing pattern, investigated more specific hypotheses about conditions leading to adolescent political rebellion. A study by Maccoby, Matthews, and Morton found that rebellion was least likely to take place among youths who reported that their parents had "about an average amount to say" regarding their activities, and was most likely to occur among both the youths who reported much parental control and those who reported being left on their own.[19] Nogee and Levin, on the contrary, found that, "although a small number do 'revolt' against their parents' political views, there is no evidence that the likelihood of such revolt is related to the strictness of parental control."[20] Middleton and Putney, in still another study of American youth's political rebellion, found limited support for their hypothesis that deviation from parental political viewpoints is related to estrangement between offspring and parent. These

[18] Robert E. Lane, "Fathers and Sons: Foundations of Political Belief," *American Sociological Review*, XXIV (1959), pp. 502–511.

[19] Eleanor E. Maccoby, Richard E. Matthews, and Anton S. Morton, "Youth and Political Change," *Public Opinion Quarterly*, XVIII (1954), pp. 23–39.

[20] Phillip Nogee and Murray B. Levin, "Some Determinants of Political Attitudes Among College Voters," *Public Opinion Quarterly*, XXII (1958), pp. 449–463.

relationships, however, occurred only when the parent was interested in politics. They stress that the relationships are not very strong and that adolescent rebellion is not an important source of political attitudes in American society.[21]

These studies were conducted in the American society — in the context of a permissive family structure and a relatively stable political and social system. Adolescent rebellion may well be more common in other societies, especially those in which the family structure is more authoritarian and rebellion against parents is more necessary to maturation, and in those countries in which rapid social and political change cause tensions between generations. The latter condition we would expect to be particularly important. In modernizing societies, for example, it is probably not uncommon for adolescents and young adults to break with the traditional orientations of parents and to adopt different, more "modern" social and political orientations. This form of rebellion against parents may be promoted by the schools, occupational organizations, and peer groups which serve as socializing agents for the modernizing forces. Political, social, and economic modernizing forces often occur as a challenge to the ideas and the power position of the traditionally oriented family. Modern perspectives may, at the same time, be very appealing to the young. The rebellion of the young against family authority, and at least a temporary lessening of the family's influence in political socialization, may be the result of such a confrontation.[22]

These phenomena are probably common in societies experiencing conflict between traditional social patterns and various centralizing, modernizing, nationalizing, and industrializing forces — a condition prevalent in a large part of the world today. The 1930's study of Bennington College girls found changes in political and social attitudes during college years, suggesting that extensive deviation of youth from parental orientations can occur even in American society when contrary pressures are harmonious (*i.e.*, peer and educational institution) and when social unrest and change are widespread.[23]

[21] Middleton and Putney, *loc. cit.*
[22] Davies, *op. cit.*, p. 17.
[23] Theodore M. Newcomb, *Personality and Social Change* (New York: Dryden Press, 1943).

Other aspects of family structure and family relationships are also related to political socialization patterns. One such factor is the absence of the father in the family unit. A number of studies have indicated that the absence of the father — either altogether in a physical sense or present but not performing a paternal role — has important consequences for the socialization of children.[24] Kenneth Langton, in a study of political socialization in Jamaica, compared the political socialization effect of maternal families with that of two-parent families.[25] He found that children in families without a father tended to be more authoritarian, to be less interested in politics, and to have a lower sense of political efficacy. The father's absence seemed to have a more pronounced effect upon boys than girls, and the relationships generally held true for families of different social classes. The father seems to serve as the more important socializing figure within these families, and his presence or absence makes a difference in whether the offspring will be politically aware. Langton also reports that in those families in which both parents were present, the father rather than the mother was chosen as a source of political advice and influence by more than two-thirds of the children.

THE FAMILY IN POLITICAL SOCIALIZATION

Though a comprehensive statement of the family role in political socialization is not possible, the primary propositions of this chapter should be clear. The family is one of the key structures through which political socialization occurs. Its influence is particularly strong in establishing basic political loyalties and attachments to the political system as a whole, to its structures and symbols, and to various groups which make up the society. The family's influence depends both on the relationship between the family and other agents of political learning and on the internal structure of the family and its own efforts at political socialization.

The fact that much political learning occurs through the

24 See, for example, David B. Lynn and William L. Sawrey, "The Effects of Father Absence on Norwegian Boys and Girls," *Journal of Abnormal and Social Psychology*, LIX (September 1959), pp. 258–262.

25 Kenneth P. Langton, "The Political Socialization Process: The Case of Secondary School Students in Jamaica" (unpublished Ph.D. dissertation, University of Oregon, 1965), pp. 115–117.

family, rather than through more specifically political and more predominantly secondary structures, has great importance for the formation of the political culture and its relationship with the political order. Though a number of consequences were suggested above, it is useful to review these notions, and to view them more systematically in the context of the family's socialization role.

The most obvious result of the dominant role of the family in basic political learning is the diffuse and decentralized form that political socialization takes. Within the society, political socialization is carried out by thousands, and in some societies millions, of separate units, which are only indirectly related to each other or to any central social force or agent. The family is beyond the direct control of any centralized agency and so is free to carry out political socialization efforts, or (perhaps equally important) not to transmit political orientations, pretty much at will.

Families perform political socialization as one of their least conscious and deliberate functions. A good deal of the political learning that takes place through the family occurs without systematic planning, organization, or intention. It is, more often than not, incidental to other activities carried out within the family. Political training is rarely recognized by the family as a major task or objective. Families generally work hard to prepare their children for marriage, child rearing and homemaking and employment. Only rarely do they exert much deliberate effort to prepare them for citizenship status.

This state of diffusion exists even in opposition to the wishes of the political leadership. Even if centralized political leaders sought to manipulate totally the processes and content of political learning, they would find it impossible to ensure that each family would transmit the "right" political examples, and that it would not pass on "wrong" views. Primary relationships like those found in the family are at the same time the most potent in influencing and motivating human behavior, and the most difficult to create or inhibit from the outside. These factors render *much* of the most important socializing experiences free from manipulation by any centralized institutions, political or otherwise. This, of course, does not mean that there will not be variations in the amount of centralized influence exercised over the political learning taking place within the family. Some governments, such as Communist Russia and China, attempt to exercise more control over the processes and content of family relationships than do others. There are severe limitations upon how much effective control a government can exercise over the family, and this fact very strongly affects the performance of political socialization.

Family socialization also contributes to heterogeneity or variation in a political culture. Families differ from each other. They are set in varying strata in a variety of different social structures. Members of different families consequently view the world, including the political world, from different perspectives. These varying perspectives mean different political cognitions, attitudes, and values. The offspring of different families will develop different types of political orientation as a result of family influence. Family socialization, in this way, perpetuates diverse social and political viewpoints.

Political antagonisms, loyalties, and viewpoints of both contemporary and past generations are passed down through the family — sometimes even after they have lost all other relevance for the political world. This is particularly important for the peculiar orientations of various social class, religious, and ethnic groupings. Such orientations are passed on from generation to generation through potent family socialization, and are often able to withstand pressures from the larger society for change and conformity. An interesting example of this phenomenon is the persistence of traditional party loyalties in some areas of the United States. In much of the Midwest, party loyalties in some rural areas still follow those established by the original settlement patterns in the early and mid-nineteenth century. Party loyalties of the population vary from county to county depending on whether the area was settled originally by migrants from New England or from the South. These variations in party preferences often have little or no relationship to contemporary socioeconomic relationships or political issues. They are residual loyalties, based on factors important in a previous era, which have been passed on from generation to generation through family political socialization. Similar patterns, following ethnic, national, religious, linguistic, and tribal groupings, exist in most societies. These factors, along with the differing socialization and politicization efforts of families, make it difficult to develop a completely homogeneous political culture.

The notion of differentiation in the content of family socialization should not be overstated. Though the individual family units have considerable autonomy in their performance of political socialization, they operate within a political community with a given political culture, and some sort of common history and traditions. The family's socialization task is to pass on to its offspring knowledge and values concerning its particular political culture. The family picks up the political views it passes on to its members from the political institutions and culture, from particular subcultures, and from other agents of socialization. The political society provides fairly concrete boundaries for the content of family socialization. Thus, in most societies there is a tendency toward common political education among the many family units. Differences among families will be most pronounced under conditions of social and political change and in societies characterized by extensive social and political cleavages. Over the years, and during stable periods, the movement is toward homogeneity, although complete homogeneity, as we have stressed, is probably never attained.

The prevalence of the family as a central socializing agent also tends to make political socialization a decidedly conservative or preserving force. The family, in part because of its multigenerational membership, tends to be a conserving rather than an initiating force. More than most other structures, it attempts to preserve and perpetuate traditional practices and modes of thought. Because of this conservative bias, political socialization through the family inhibits rapid and widespread common changes in political orientation, and the ability of a political culture to adjust to immediate political, social, and economic changes. This factor is a primary source of the lag that often occurs between political structures and processes on the one hand and the political culture on the other. Political institutions may be altered, sometimes very rapidly and substantially, but family units persist in passing down political attitudes appropriate to previous circumstances.

This conservative family influence can be most dramatically witnessed today in those areas of the world undergoing rapid social and political change, and particularly those polities engaged in the tedious process of nation building. Robert LeVine outlines this problem quite well.[26] LeVine is concerned particularly with the problems faced by the new nations of Africa and Asia in their attempts to develop orientations that fit new political institutions. These efforts are greatly inhibited by the fact that basic political socialization, *i.e.,* the development of fundamental political loyalties, takes place during childhood and largely in the context of the family. This factor means, first, that these polities come into existence with large numbers of adults whose political loyalties are directed toward structures other than the new nation-state, and that these basic orientations developed in childhood are very difficult to alter. Furthermore, the important role of the family makes it difficult to alter these orientations over short periods of time. Families in these areas persist in socializing their children into the traditional patterns and political structures, generally involving basic political loyalties to local tribes and local governmental units. These family socialization patterns are both slow to change and very difficult to manipulate from above.

Because of the family's predominant role, the early acquisition of basic political loyalties, and the tendency of the family to persist in traditional patterns and outlooks, basic mass political orientations will usually be altered only over long periods of time — such alterations will probably involve several generations and extensive efforts on the part of secondary instruments of political socialization, especially the schools, the mass media, and various government oriented secondary organizations. Political and social instability, resulting in part from this time lag in socialization, will most likely be common in many of the new nations for some time to come. The Soviet

26 Robert LeVine, "Political Socialization and Culture Change," in Clifford Geertz (ed.), *Old Societies and New States* (New York: The Free Press, 1963), pp. 280–304.

Union, China, and other nations that have attempted to "Sovietize" their peoples have been confronted with similar problems resulting from family socialization influences. They have attempted to handle the problem by undermining the influence of the family, and by carrying on massive socialization and resocialization efforts through schools, youth organizations, and other secondary groups manipulated by the government. There is now some indication that in the Soviet Union this family "socialization lag" has been passed and the government is shifting back to supporting and strengthening the influence of the family. This probably means that, after fifty years, the government feels that the political orientations contained within the family are now congruent with the political order, and that the family will pass on political values that are appropriate for the Soviet state.

CHAPTER VIII

Peer Groups

PEER GROUPS AND SOCIETY

The family is not the only primary group which serves as an agent of political socialization. A variety of peer groups is important in political learning. Peer groups, as we specified in Chapter VII, are a form of primary group composed of members sharing relatively equal status and intimate ties. Childhood play groups, friendship cliques, small work groups, brothers and sisters, married couples are the most common types of peer groups.

Peer groups are a basic form of social relationship and serve as important instruments of social learning and adjustment in all societies. Their prevalence and significance as agents of socialization, however, vary from culture to culture. Recent social commentators have pointed out that peer groups have become more widespread and more important as agents of socialization in modern, highly developed societies. David Riesman, and his co-authors make this point strongly in *The Lonely Crowd*.[1] They point out that peer groups are replacing parents and other authority figures as the most significant agents of socialization. Individuals in developed societies increasingly look toward peers, rather than to their elders and social authorities, for cues regarding social and political be-

[1] David Riesman, Reuel Denney, and Nathan Glazer, *The Lonely Crowd* (New Haven: Yale University Press, 1950).

havior. This trend, they argue, is a central feature of general developments taking place in modern societies.

In his book *From Generation to Generation,* S. N. Eisenstadt argues in a similar vein that peer groups, or "age-homogeneous groups" as he calls them, are necessary supplements to the family for socialization in complex modern societies.[2] Age-homogeneous groups take on increased significance for socialization because parents are not able to prepare their offspring successfully for full social status and participation in the complex and depersonalized structures found in modern societies. Unlike primitive societies, modern states are not based on kinship ties or other personalized arrangements. Because the political and social systems are not based on, or modeled after, the family structure, the family is a less suitable training ground for participation in society. Consequently, age-homogeneous groups play more significant socializing roles.[3]

This notion is related to the propositions on incomplete childhood socialization in Chapter IV, and to the argument suggesting greater discontinuity in political learning in more highly developed societies presented in Chapter VI. In more highly developed societies — those in which social and political structures less closely resemble family structures — childhood play groups, adolescent gangs and youth organizations, and adult work, social, and civic groups assume important socializing roles. Primary relationships outside the family play a greater role in preparing, motivating, and shaping individuals for participation in society.

Although we stress the growing importance of peer groups in the highly developed societies, the emphasis does not imply that such groups have no importance for socialization in other types of cultures. Youth and adult peer relationships affect social learning in even the most simple and primitive societies. Their influence, however, is not as great as in more highly developed societies because of the more pervasive and continuing influence of the family, the greater congruence between

[2] S. N. Eisenstadt, *From Generation to Generation* (New York: The Free Press, 1956).

[3] *Ibid.,* p. 54.

family and social structures, and the smaller number outside the family.

Peer groups begin to take on special importance during early adolescence, and continue to have significant influence throughout adulthood. Talcott Parsons suggests that peer groups become important socializing agents during the high school years.[4] During this period parents and school teachers as authority figures, cue givers, and transmitters of social learning diminish in importance. Cliques, youth gangs, and other youth groups become influential. In a study of American youth culture James Coleman carefully documents the proposition that during the adolescent period peers replace parents or teachers as the most significant reference figures.[5] This is but the beginning of peer group influence, however. Peer relationships continue as important socializing agents throughout the adult period. Their form changes to marriage and other family peer relationships, to work and professional colleagues, to neighborhood associates, and to primary relationships contained in religious and social organizations.

PEER GROUPS AND POLITICAL LEARNING

In pointing to the growing significance of peer groups, these studies do not deal with the specific issue of political socialization. However, inasmuch as the form and process of political learning parallel other forms of social learning, these patterns can be assumed to hold for political socialization. Peer groups are important agencies through which political orientations are transmitted, nurtured, and altered. Their role becomes particularly important for adolescent and adult political learning. Family influence wanes and various peer groups become significant as agents of political socialization, approximately when the establishment of basic political orientations and knowledge have been fairly well accomplished — at about age 13 or 14. This is also the point in the life cycle when persons

[4] Talcott Parsons, "The School Class as a Social System: Some of Its Functions in American Society," *Harvard Education Review*, XXIX (1959), pp. 297–318.

[5] James S. Coleman, *The Adolescent Society* (New York: The Free Press, 1961).

begin to take on more active interest and participation in specifically political affairs — when they begin to anticipate and in some instances assume adult political roles. The correspondence between stages in the development of the political self, the relative impact of different agents of political socialization, and the assumption of adult political roles, has important consequences for the types of political learning for which peer relationships are most important.

In the preceding chapter, we said that the parental family plays its most important role in the establishment of basic political loyalties, identifications, and perceptions. Parents pass on such fundamental orientations as national identification, political party identifications, identification with social groups, and the acceptance or rejection of political processes, institutions, and procedures. These political orientations are acquired primarily during childhood, and largely within the context of the family and the school. We have stressed also that political socialization does, and indeed must, continue throughout life. It is not concluded with the acquisition of basic political attachments and knowledge. It is rarely possible for the family and childhood socializing experiences, of even the most efficient and thorough form, to prepare the individual completely for all conditions he confronts in the political world. With adulthood, new orientations often are developed and different political roles are assumed.

The interpretation of and adjustment to political changes, and the preparation for participation in specifically political roles are the basic task of late adolescent and adult political socialization. It is during these particular stages that peer group socialization is most significant. Much of the form and content of peer group political learning is, for this reason, different from that of early childhood. The later political learning may serve to alter or reinforce earlier political learning. Where early political socialization was insufficient, peer group socialization as well as other types of adult political learning may contribute to the acquisition of the more basic political orientations. As a rule, however, late adolescent and adult peer group socialization serves primarily to supplement the basic political learning, and to prepare the individual for more specific political experiences. Peer groups provide continuing cues through which individuals understand and adjust to everyday changes in the political world.

Particularly in more stable polities, the specifically directed orientations that are acquired later are generally built upon views acquired in childhood. Reactions to specific political events and adjustments to political changes reflect institutional and group identifications and the general social and political values acquired during early socializing experiences. For example, positions adopted by citizens on specific policy issues tend to be based upon identification with liberal, conservative, socialist, capitalist, anticolonialist, or other political symbols. In a similar manner adult support or opposition to political leaders is often based upon identification with racial, linguistic, religious, ethnic, regional, or tribal groupings developed early in life.

In instances where the individual, the political community, or both, have experienced significant changes, political references acquired in childhood may prove irrelevant, and later socialization experiences will substantially alter basic political attachments and interpretations. Under such circumstances, peer groups can be a source of discontinuities in political learning, as well as the means through which individuals adjust to changes in the political world. The peasant who moves to the city, the African tribesman who finds himself a part of a new nation-state, and the urbanite who moves up in occupational status and out to the suburbs may change their political orientations. In alterations such as these new peer groups — new work and neighborhood associates — often act as transmitters of attitudes appropriate for the new social positions. Given the amount of individual mobility and the extent and rapidity of change in the contemporary world, this type of "resocialization" is widespread.

THE SOURCES OF PEER GROUP INFLUENCE

The particularly potent socializing influence of peer groups stems from the same two factors that make the family so important. These are: (1) the extensive access of peer groups to their members and (2) the emotionally laden, personal rela-

tionships that exist within them. Peer groups provide members
with considerable access and exposure to each other. Such
groups command a degree of attention from members that
secondary groups and communication media rarely obtain.
Access and attentiveness are, of course, major requisites for
socialization. Without adequate communication and attention
to that communication a group cannot transmit political
orientations or shape political behavior. Although adolescent
and adult peer groups rarely possess the nearly monopolistic
access that the family has to the infant and young child, they
have considerable personal contact — more than most secondary structures. Friends, family members, and close work associates are effective socializing agents, in large part, because
they are both available and heeded.

In addition to a high level of interaction among the members, peer groups are characterized by highly personal and
emotionally involved relationships. We know that political
socialization, like other kinds of socialization, is facilitated by
the emotional strength of interpersonal relationships. Those
groups and individuals with whom one is most deeply involved
have the greatest impact upon the development and stability
of one's political self. Interpersonal relationships or personal
influences, such as those occurring in both family and peer
types of primary groups, are among the most significant factors
in the development and maintenance of social and political
orientations. The influence of interpersonal relationships has
been the object of considerable investigation in recent years.
A book summarizing much of this literature is *Personal Influence* by Katz and Lazarsfeld. In analyzing the impact of personal influence on attitudes and values they state that:
"Interpersonal relationships seem to be *'anchorage' points for
individual opinions, attitudes, habits, and values.*" [6] They
stress that interpersonal influences remain extremely important even in the midst of extensive mass media and numerous
secondary structures.

The theory and data documenting the influence of primary
groups on individual behavior is one of the most systematically

[6] Elihu Katz and Paul F. Lazarsfeld, *Personal Influence* (New York: The
Free Press, 1955), p. 44.

developed bodies of propositions found in contemporary social science. Study after study has shown that members of small groups tend to think and act alike, and that the bulk of an individual's values are grounded in his network of primary relationships. A review by Cartwright and Zander offers three general explanatory hypotheses concerning the sources of primary group impact: (1) "Membership in a group determines to a great extent many of the things a person will learn, see, experience, or think about," (2) "An individual may act like other members of a group because they are attractive to him and he wants to be like them," and (3) "A person may act like other members of a group because he fears punishment, ridicule or rejection by the rest of the group if he does not." [7]

Peer groups affect individual political orientations in a number of ways. First, as Cartwright and Zander suggest, they are among the most important sources of information and attitudes about the social and political worlds. A substantial part of a person's social learning is filtered through his various primary relationships. This point is both quite evident and extremely important for comprehending the socializing impact of small groups. Very simply, peer groups serve as communication channels through which knowledge and norms are communicated and evaluated. In much the same way as the family is the major channel through which the young child learns about the social environment beyond his immediate family, peer groups are channels through which individuals acquire knowledge about their political world during later life. They are important and successful as communication channels precisely because of their basic attributes of frequent and attentive access and personal relationships.

The proposition concerning the potent role of primary groups as communication channels has received systematic treatment in mass media research. Communications from the media flow through networks of personal relationships. Communications flow not so much directly from media to individuals, but in a two-step flow from the mass media to some few

[7] Dorwin Cartwright and Alvin Zander, "Group Pressures and Group Standards: Introduction," in Cartwright and Zander (eds.), *Group Dynamics: Research and Theory* (New York: Harper, 1960), p. 169.

individuals (opinion leaders), and then to other individuals among whom there are close ties. Primary groups intervene between mass media and the populations to which the media are directed. Several studies of American voting behavior suggest that this intervening role is prevalent in the communication of political messages and the formation of individual political decisions.[8]

In a closely related but more fundamental sense, primary groups help equip the individual with his special conception of the political world, a part of which may be termed his social reality. The individual tends to view the social world, including the world of politics, through the context of his primary relationships. In early life the family, and in later years adolescent and adult peer groups provide the individual, not only with important communication links, but also with his very conceptualization of self and his position in the social world. A number of studies have stressed how extensively individual perceptions of self and the world are determined by particular group relationships.[9] As Festinger, Schachter, and Back point out: "The hypothesis may be advanced that the 'social reality' upon which an opinion or an attitude rests for its justification is the degree to which the individual perceives that this opinion or attitude is shared by others. An opinion or attitude which is not reinforced by others of the same opinion will become unstable generally." [10] Peer groups, then, provide the individual with much of his interpretation and understanding of the political world and how he fits into it — his political self.

Peer groups also socialize individuals by motivating or pressuring them to conform to attitudes and behavior accepted by the group. On the one hand, peer groups serve as reference figures. Individuals adopt the views of their close associates

[8] Paul F. Lazarsfeld, Bernard Berelson, and Hazel Gaudet, *The People's Choice* (New York: Columbia University Press, 1948), and Bernard Berelson, Paul F. Lazarsfeld, and William N. McPhee, *Voting* (Chicago: University of Chicago Press, 1954).

[9] Reports of some of these studies can be found in Cartwright and Zander, *op. cit.*, Part 3.

[10] Leon Festinger, Stanley Schachter, and Kurt Back, *Social Pressures in Informal Groups* (New York: Harper, 1950), p. 168.

because they like or respect them, or because they want to be like them. An individual may develop an interest in politics and come to follow political events simply because his close friends or work associates do. He models his interests and behavior after theirs. The high school or college graduate moving into a wage-earning position, the country-reared laborer moving into an industrial job in the city, and the city-raised youth moving into a professional status and out to the suburbs may adopt the norms of his new work associates in an effort to be accepted by them.

In other instances peer groups pressure members into accepting their orientations and behavior by threatening to punish deviation from group norms. Such pressures may be subtle and informal, such as ridiculing the deviant or being less responsive to him. Or they may be more explicit and blatant, such as depriving deviant members of group rewards or even of group membership. In primary groups even very subtle forms of disapproval or ridicule are effective as instruments for motivating or restricting behavior. Similarly, group praise and reinforcement can serve as an effective socializing mechanism. The close, personal ties mean that members are extremely sensitive to group pressures. This renders their rewards and punishments extremely potent as socializing instruments.

The impact of peer groups on specifically political orientations and behavior has received only scant attention, unfortunately. Berelson and his co-authors, in their study of how voters made their decisions in the 1948 presidential election, investigated the influence of two types of peer groups, friends and work associates.[11] They collected information on their respondents' closest friends and three closest work associates, on the assumption that these were the most important peer relationships. The voter was usually tied in with a network of personal associations that were both homogeneous and congenial. The correspondence among friends was slightly stronger than that among work associates. Democrats tended to have predominantly Democratic friends and coworkers, and Republicans to have mainly Republican associates. These rela-

11 Berelson, Lazarsfeld, and McPhee, *op. cit.*, p. 94.

tionships were increasingly stronger for older voters. Young voters were less likely to have friends and coworkers who shared voting preferences and party identifications. At the same time, young voters were more likely than older voters to have political preferences similar to those of their parents. As the voter grows older the relative influence of peer associates increases, while that of the family decreases.

> Thus, the political conviction of the individual is closely bound to the political character of his personal relations — or at least his perception of their political complexion. A sense of security about one's judgment seems to be a function of the congeniality of the personal environment; here, as elsewhere in the realm of political attitudes and behavior, the private political conscience of the citizen rests upon a near-by group norm represented by the people around him. Without their support it is not easy to hold strong political attitudes, and relatively few people do.[12]

The 1952 and 1956 election studies, conducted by the Survey Research Center, offer similar evidence regarding the homogeneity of political orientations among peer associates.[13] In the 1952 study a series of questions was asked about the voting preferences of spouses, three closest friends, and work associates.[14] High correspondence was found among all three of these peer groups, with spouses ranking highest, friends second, and work associates third. Voters from homogeneous groups share the political preferences of that group. The influence of peer associates is even more strongly suggested by what happens when friends and coworkers are evenly divided. In the absence of harmonious preferences among friends, voters show little tendency to lean one way or the other. Voting preferences of divided work associates parallel fairly closely those of the total voting population.

A study of the political party preferences of Swedish young men provides additional evidence of the same relationships.[15] This study reports "a singularly close association between the

12 *Ibid.*, p. 96.

13 Angus Campbell, *et al.*, *The American Voter* (New York: Wiley, 1960), and Angus Campbell, *et al.*, *The Voter Decides* (New York: Harper, 1954).

14 Angus Campbell, *et al.*, *The Voter Decides, op. cit.*, pp. 199–206.

15 Georg Karlsson, "Political Attitudes Among Male Swedish Youth," *Acta Sociologica*, III (1958), pp. 220–241.

political opinions of the friends and the individual's own opinion when the views held by the friends on political matters are uniform, and this association is closest when all three friends are perceived to hold identical opinions." [16]

These studies, along with other research on the effect of small groups on social attitudes and behavior, offer support for several propositions about the relative influence of a peer group on the political orientations of its members. *First,* the peer associates are more likely to influence the individual when the group members are in agreement. Groups with divided or conflicting political orientations are less likely to influence an individual's political predispositions effectively than are harmonious groups. *Second,* peer groups are most likely to serve as agents of political socialization when politics is important to the group and when the group deliberately attempts to convey political norms. *Third,* the influence of a peer group on an individual is determined in part by the strength of that individual's ties with the group. The more important the group is to an individual, the more likely he is to be influenced. These propositions, the reader may notice, are similar to those suggested in the last chapter to explain the differential influence of families as agents of political socialization.

Peer groups are probably the most effective political socialization agents in later life. Generally, they are more effective than other adult institutions in communicating political norms, motivating political behavior, and enforcing adherence to chosen political ideas. Peer groups, however, do not operate in isolation from each other or from other types of social structures. In forming, reinforcing, and adjusting orientations, primary groups serve also to link the individual with the less personal groups and structures. They operate not as self-contained systems, but as links which connect the individual with other more inclusive and less concrete social networks. Berelson, Lazarsfeld, and McPhee state this idea as follows:

> Actually, friends and co-workers serve less as closed cliques than as contact points through whom the individual is connected to

[16] *Ibid.,* p. 225.

whole networks of social relations that affect political behavior.
The networks are organized in major socio-economic and ethnic
blocs, and at their center are the main institutions of the community and its ultimate leadership. Thus, one's personal associates are not distinct entities from class and ethnic strata but
rather connect the individual to others in such strata.[17]

This point is extremely important for understanding the complete structure of socialization, as well as how primary groups
fit into the overall content.

If we are to understand social learning fully, we must recognize the way in which groups like the family and peer groups
combine with secondary groups to affect the maturing citizen.
The primary units transmit and enforce the orientations of
particular structures with which they are related; the secondary groups provide the social and political context for the
primary groups. Primary relationships, thus, both draw individuals into more general groups and transmit the political
outlooks of these groups to the individual. We have commented briefly on the intermediary role that personal relationships play in the flow and interpretation of mass communication
messages. They play a similar role for other secondary groups.
A citizen often learns the political norms of his ethnic, occupational, religious, or tribal group from primary groups that
exist within the larger group. The Jew in the Western world,
the Indian in East Africa, and the Chinese scattered throughout Asia establish identity with their particular ethnic group
and learn its political values, through the family and other
close associates who are part of the group. In the same way, in
a large labor union with stated political values and objectives,
these ideas and norms are probably most successfully communicated by the many small work groups making up the
union.

Two exceptions to the general patterns should be recognized. The social backgrounds of close associates are conse-
quential for the role of primary relationships in political
socialization after childhood. If adult associates are of a social
and economic background similar to that of an individual's
family, they are likely to reinforce the political learning that

[17] Berelson, Lazarsfeld, and McPhee, *op. cit.*, p. 94.

took place in the family during an earlier period. On the other hand, if they are not like the individual family, they are most likely to alter his previous political learning.

Further, adults, especially in complex societies, belong to numerous peer groups. Family peers, work associates, school friends, and neighborhood associates form important but different primary groups. An individual develops primary associates within almost any social structure or secondary group to which he belongs. Various peer groups may offer similar or conflicting political cues to the same individual. The general tendency is for political and social pressures of one's various primary associates to be harmonious and consistent. In large part this is so because primary associations are tied in with the broader and politically significant social structures. Even in fairly heterogeneous societies personal associates commonly are drawn from the same social class, ethnic association, and religious, racial, and linguistic affiliation. These basic social positions are established primarily through the family. Because various social activities within a social category, are related to each other and because one usually chooses associates who are similar in background, peer groups are more likely to reinforce each other. This is an important source of the strength and stability of many political orientations.

This mutual reinforcement by different peer groups, and the stability that follows from it are, of course, less prevalent in societies with extensive social and geographic mobility and those experiencing rapid change. Social and geographic mobility are likely to lead the individual to peer relationships tied in with different social classes, ethnic groupings, etc.; to make him the recipient of conflicting political cues. The individual moving from farm to city, from a lower class neighborhood to an upper income community, from a low status job to a high status one, or vice versa, may maintain close associates within both groupings. Friends in the different social groups will exert conflicting political pressures. This type of cross-pressure from a number of primary groups is similar to the pressures that often exist between the family and peer groups during late adolescence and early adulthood. When such conflicts occur individuals generally follow the influence of the group most important to them, those with whom they are most intimately related, or those most politically relevant.

POLITICAL SOCIALIZATION AND THE
INFLUENCE OF PEER GROUPS

We have pointed out in this chapter that peer groups are important agents of political learning, that they are generally most influential during adolescence and adulthood, and that consequently they have their major influence at the later stages of political maturation. We have also suggested that peer groups become more significant in political and social learning as nations become more industrial and urban.

With respect to the consequences of peer group socialization for the overall structure of political learning, peer groups are like families in some ways and not like them in other ways. Like the family, peer groups make the process of political learning haphazard, nondeliberate, and largely decentralized. As it does in the family, political learning takes place and political values are transmitted as a secondary consequence of other, more important activities. A small group of close friends who gather to play poker every Thursday night, or neighboring farmers or peasants who go to the local tavern on Saturday night, may become involved in political discussions. When they get together, they sometimes talk about politics; they influence each other's political values. In this capacity the poker playing group and the Saturday evening drinking group operate as agents of political socialization. This, however, is an unintended consequence of their getting together. It does not diminish the influence of peer groups on political orientations, but it does mean that the effect is not systematic, regular, or certain.

Peer group influence, also like that of the family, is generally free from overall centralized control. Any central agency, public or private, that attempts to manipulate the content of political learning, is likely to be frustrated by its inability to control the socialization taking place in peer groups. We elaborated this argument previously in regard to the family. Here, we add that similar conditions affect peer groups.

We also suggested in Chapter VII that the effect of the family's critical role as a socialization agency is to make political socialization a generally conservative force. There is in the family a bias toward continuity from one generation to the next, a tendency to pass on and maintain traditional values even after they have been discarded by more centrally controlled agents of political learning. This tendency is probably less characteristic of peer group socialization, although the peer group's impact will depend ultimately upon which of many different structures the peer group is tied in with. Their significant influence may be in the opposite direction from the conservative influence of the family. That is to say, peer groups are likely to facilitate changes in political orientation, rather than work against them. This is so because peer groups serve as agents of political learning for the most part later in life, when the major influence of the family has passed and the individual is establishing a more direct and participating relationship with the political world.

As with so many aspects of political socialization, this pattern can be seen most vividly in societies experiencing large-scale change, especially in the new nations. In many of several dozen nations in the contemporary world, the peasant child acquires from his family a traditional political outlook, even after the institutions and goals of the polity have been substantially altered. This is, of course, what we mean when we refer to the conservative influence of the family. Let us say that the young peasant leaves the family and the village. He goes off to school, to work in a city, to serve in the armed forces. Here he is confronted with a different set of political realities and political values. He is also likely to form new primary relationships outside the family, to join new peer groups. These new-found peers are likely to influence his political and social values. And, more important, in the developing societies they are likely to influence him to adopt values consistent with the contemporary political world. They play a major part in helping him adjust to a new political order, by altering the traditional political outlook established in his family. In this situation, then, peer groups help to change political orientations rather than to conserve old ones.

One of the most comprehensive studies of the influence of peer groups in contributing to political change is the Bennington College study by Newcomb. This study analyzed the liberalization of political attitudes of college girls from conservative homes during their four years at Bennington College during the 1930's. On the whole there was a marked change in most of the girls in party preferences and political attitudes over their college years. Most of them started out conservative and Republican and ended as political liberals or radicals. The general climate of the college was liberal, and at least during the college term the girls were relatively isolated from other sources of political and social influence. The reasons for these changes are complex. From our standpoint, one of the most important findings was that those girls who established close personal ties with their college peers and accepted fellow students as reference groups were more likely to alter their political outlooks than those who maintained their closest ties with parents and looked toward their family as their major reference group. It was the peer groups that altered the political views developed in the family.

Peer groups, of course, can have the opposite effect. They may inhibit changes or adjustments in political outlook. In fact, the key to understanding the persistence of minority groups which maintain traditional political values lies in the influence of peer groups. One of the major strategies of most such groups is to limit the basis of primary relationships. There is usually an effort to see that close personal relationships are developed only with other group members, and to inhibit close contact, or at least close personal relationships with nongroup members.

In general, though, we suspect that the overall influence of peer groups is to facilitate adjustments in political outlooks as the citizen confronts the changing political world. Peer groups are critical forces in maintaining the complex balance between stability and change in political orientations so important for both the individual and the political community.

CHAPTER IX

Education, the Schools, and Political Learning

EDUCATION AND SCHOOLING: AN OVERVIEW

Schooling, be it in a jungle, a field, or a classroom, is an experience few children in the world avoid. The years between early childhood and puberty (in nonliterate societies) and between early childhood and late adolescence (in literate societies) are given over in large part to learning the skills and values which prepare the child for adulthood. Systematic instruction in the use of the tools and the social skills necessary for effective operation in the adult world is given at this age, when the individual is more than a baby but not yet an adult. Instruction may be in the hands of teachers specially appointed to this task, or it may be left to parents or older siblings. The instruction may be organized into regular classes, or it may entail a less explicit program. The schooling may be in reading and writing, in food gathering techniques, in weapons and fighting, or in numerous other technologies and skills. However programmed, and whatever its content, schooling in the fundamentals of a society's technology is seldom left to chance.[1]

The same schooling agencies which provide the child with the fundamentals of his society's technology also help him

---

[1] Erik H. Erikson has written that all children, in all cultures, must adjust themselves to the inorganic laws of the tool world. See *Childhood and Society* (New York: Norton, 1950), Chapter 7.

acquire the cultural norms and expectations associated with membership in society. We can see this clearly in the familiar curriculum of Western schools. Civics classes are taught along with reading classes. Good conduct is instilled at the same time as good grammar. The beginning school child learns that obedience to authority is as necessary for success as is conquering the new math. The African herdsboy has a schooling which in its essential outcome is similar. The rules and regulations governing the care of the cattle are intended not only to guarantee that he knows how to keep cattle, but also to introduce him to an intricate system of cultural norms regarding the social, economic, and political life of the community. So it is across the world and through the ages — pre-adult years are a time for acquiring the tools and learning the rules which pave the way for adulthood.

We are, of course, more interested in the second half of this formula — learning the norms of the society. More narrowly still, we focus on those aspects of schooling which have consequences for political life. To avoid terminological confusion, we distinguish schooling from education on the one hand and from socialization on the other.

It is a commonplace that education and schooling are not synonymous. Society educates through a wide variety of agencies — the family, the clan elders, churches, mass media, *ad infinitum*. The classroom takes its place alongside these other educational forces. It neither replaces nor dominates them. In this chapter we will restrict ourselves to the formal educational system. In other chapters we deal with socialization as it occurs in those educational institutions not normally understood as schools.

Schooling is both broader and more narrow than socialization. It is broader in that schools perform many tasks, ranging from baby-sitting for working mothers to physical training of young men in preparation for military duties. Many of these tasks are not properly labeled as socialization. On the other hand, schooling is more narrow than socialization. We reserve the word "schooling" for the more or less conscious attempt by an older generation to instruct the young specifically through a set of institutions set aside for that purpose.

We can best understand the notion of schooling by viewing it in the context of mass public education. Allowing for considerable variation between nations, the following elements are common to public education systems: (1) tax supported public institutions explicitly charged with instructing the young in a wide variety of skills and values; (2) specially trained and recruited personnel to do the teaching; (3) more or less daily attendance during the better part of the years between the ages of six and sixteen; and (4) a more or less common curriculum so that children of the same age receive fairly similar instruction. This is, of course, a Western picture, though one not unfamiliar to African, Asian, and Latin American students. Important exceptions appear as one shifts from country to country. Some states charge school fees; in other states, the schools are totally free. In most nations there are private and parochial educational systems in addition to the public schools. These, however, are apt to follow a similar general format. Different proportions of the school age populations of different nations are actually in school. Less than 2 per cent of Uganda's late adolescents, for example, are in secondary schools, compared to 95 per cent of young people in the United States. The school curriculum in France is much more uniform than that of India, where even the language of instruction varies from area to area. Despite differences, school systems from one country to the next do have common elements, and, extrapolating from present trends, we expect increasing similarity.

Schooling is linked to the development of the political self in two distinct ways. First, schools entail political socialization experiences which shape the orientations of the preadult. The educational program provides instruction in appropriate political values. The major part of this chapter will deal with these experiences.

In addition, a person's level of education affects his way of understanding the world of politics. The highly educated generally perceive the political world and their position in it differently from those with little or no education. This results not so much from the school as transmitter of values or training ground for political life as from the fact that the educated and noneducated view society so differently. This notion will be discussed at the end of this chapter.

In most societies the school years begin at age five or six and end at 17 or 18, except for the few who continue with higher education. As we have shown in previous chapters, these years are critical for the development of the political self. We will try here to designate the mechanisms through which the educational system socializes the young people politically. To place the material that follows in perspective, the reader should keep in mind two qualifications. First, the two major agencies already discussed — the family and peer groups — operate concurrently with the school system as political socialization forces. Although during the first few years in the individual's life the family has almost exclusive influence, schools seldom have such a monopoly of access. Schools may or may not teach the same values as other socializing agents.

Second, the years between five and eighteen cover considerable ground, especially in respect to the formation of the political self. It would be preferable to show how educational experiences affect the political values of specific age groups. This has not been possible here. Frequently we are forced to speak of the "school years" or "school experiences" without distinguishing between primary and secondary years, etc. The reader should bear in mind the ideas presented in previous chapters about the differential rate and content of political socialization in different age groups.

We will discuss the influence of the school in political socialization as three major categories: (1) the influence of the classroom, focusing on the formal curriculum, the ritual life, and the teacher; (2) aspects of the school other than the formal classroom: the social climate of the school, political youth organizations, and extracurricular activities; and (3) the effect of being educated on the political self and the role of the school in relation to other agents of political socialization.

THE FORMAL CLASSROOM
AND POLITICAL SOCIALIZATION

In modern societies a major portion of political learning takes place in the classroom. It is through this agency that the most comprehensive and deliberate efforts are made by modern and modernizing polities to shape the political outlooks of new citizens. Within the classroom the formal curriculum of instruction, various ritual activities, and the activities of the teacher all help to shape the political development of youngsters.

1. *The Curriculum.* The curriculum is potentially one of the major instruments of political socialization. Its importance as an initiator and reinforcer of cultural values is well stated by Anderson and Fisher:

> The school curriculum that lies in the heart of the educational systems of western societies is one of the great cultural forms of human history. Its content embraces diverse culture traits believed to be requisite for participation in the society. . . . Many of the basic "values" of the society are to be reinforced (if not originally transmitted to pupils) by means of the choice of materials placed before them in society.[2]

Nationalistic values, in particular, permeate the entire school curriculum. Courses in national history tend to be selective: "those episodes that redound most to our national glory receive emphasis; and the picture of the past is deficient in cracks and crevices."[3] Formal instruction in civics and government is designed to acquaint the adolescent citizen with the nature and the glory of the established order. The use of literature reflects favorably on the nation's past and forecasts great things for its future. Such portrayals are presented for citizenship training. Generally political leaders and educators explicitly view the curriculum as an appropriate agency for transmitting knowledge and values conducive to good citizenship.

A distinction can be made between two types of formal political instruction: civic education and political indoctrination. The distinction is ambiguous, but will serve the purpose at hand. Following the suggestion of Coleman, we call "civic training" that part of political education which emphasizes how a good citizen participates in the political life of his nation. Political indoctrination, on the other hand, concerns the learning of a specific political ideology which is intended

[2] C. Arnold Anderson and Suellen Fisher, "The Curriculum as an Instrument for Inculcating Attitudes and Values," Comparative Education Center, University of Chicago, unpublished manuscript, 1967.

[3] V. O. Key, Jr., *Public Opinion and American Democracy* (New York: Knopf, 1961), p. 317.

to rationalize and justify a particular regime.[4] Civic training acquaints the student with a political unit toward which loyalty is assumed. Political indoctrination inculcates loyalty to the nation. All educational curricula contain a mixture of both of these objectives. A society trying to bind the people to the political community or establishing a new political order may find it beneficial to place more stress on indoctrination, and to use the curriculum to legitimate and justify as well as to instruct.

(a) *Civic training.* In an early classic study, *The Making of Citizens,* Charles Merriam observed that:

> The school emerges in recent times as the major instrument in the shaping of civic education. A process, extending over a considerable period of years, now takes the place of the week or ten days once given to the tribal candidate in his period of novitiate, and organizes and schematizes this process with great elaboration. With the development of universal education, the training is extended to the entire population, female as well as male, and the whole community is drawn into the net.[5]

Merriam summarized the findings of a survey of eight western nations. He further observed that, "In all the systems appraised in this study, the school emerges as the heart of the civic education of the political community, and in all probability will continue to function increasingly in this role." [6]

Educators, students of politics, journalists, and others have echoed Merriam for the last three and a half decades. There is no doubt that citizenship training is a part of most school curricula. There is some doubt about the influence of such programs. Some commentators, sensitive to the gap between what is taught in the school and what the child learns outside the classroom, play down the influence of such attempts at civic training.

An anthropological study of Peyrane, a French village in the

---

[4] See James S. Coleman (ed.), *Education and Political Development* (Princeton: Princeton University Press, 1965), p. 226.

[5] Charles E. Merriam, *The Making of Citizens* (Chicago: University of Chicago Press, 1931), p. 273.

[6] *Ibid.*, p. 288.

Vaucluse, is worth citing in this context.[7] Laurence Wylie reports that the core curriculum in the local school includes various civics courses. Students memorize sentences which stress the benevolent, disinterested nature of the government. But parents and teachers speak a different language when they talk about the government. The attitude caught when the children overhear adults "is in direct conflict with what the children are taught in school."[8] From listening to the grownups, children learn that government is made up of "weak, stupid, selfish, ambitious men."[9] No matter what image the children read about in their civics textbooks, they "constantly hear adults referring to Government as a source of evil and to the men who run it as instruments of evil."[10] They further learn that it is the "duty of the citizen *not* to cooperate with these men, as the civics books would have people do, but rather to hinder them, to prevent them in every possible way from increasing their power over individuals and over families."[11] This is a picture of incongruity, in which the content of the formal school curriculum is probably superseded by informal learning experiences.

For most students the discrepancy between curriculum materials, other political cues, and actual political experiences is not as severe. When the textbook portrays a political world which is confirmed by his own observation, or by what is transmitted by other socialization agents, the student is likely to be more receptive to its political lessons. A study of civic training in several American high schools confirms this notion.[12] This study, conducted by Edgar Litt, found that the curriculum did affect the kinds of political values developed by students. The influence was accelerated when the values being taught were in harmony with those articulated by other

7 Laurence Wylie, *Village in the Vaucluse* (Cambridge, Mass.: Harvard University Press, 1957).

8 *Ibid.*, p. 206.

9 *Ibid.*, p. 207.

10 *Ibid.*, p. 208.

11 *Ibid.*, p. 207.

12 Edgar Litt, "Civic Education, Community Norms, and Political Indoctrination," *American Sociological Review*, XXVIII (1963), pp. 69–75. Reprinted in Litt (ed.), *The Political Imagination* (Glenview, Ill.: Scott, Foresman, 1966), pp. 487–494.

socialization agents. It was attenuated, however, where the textbook values were out of line with the norms of other, more powerful, agents of political learning.

Litt analyzed textbooks used in a civic education course and reported that the emphasis on the democratic creed — "The rights of citizens and minorities to attempt to influence governmental policy through nontyrannical procedures" — overwhelmed all other political messages. Table IX.1 summarizes some of these findings. Litt went on to compare these norms with the values articulated by teachers, PTA officials, school administrators, and religious, civic, and political leaders in the community. He found considerable congruence between the civics textbooks and these other community cue givers.[13]

TABLE IX.1 *References on Salient Political Dimensions in Civics Textbooks (number of paragraphs analyzed: 1335)*

Political dimension	Percentage
Emphasis on democratic creed	52
Chauvinistic references to American political institutions	4
Emphasis on political activity, citizen's duty, efficacy	12
Emphasis on political process, politicians, and power	5
Emphasis on group conflict — resolving political functions	4
Other (descriptive references)	23

Source: This table is computed from one presented in Edgar Litt (ed.), *The Political Imagination* (Glenview, Ill.: Scott, Foresman, 1966), p. 489.

Exposure to a civics education program did alter basic attitudes about politics. Students who took the course showed strengthened "support for democratic processes."[14] They were most affected by themes presented in the civic education program and supported by attitudes of community leaders. On the other hand, the civics education curriculum *did not affect* attitudes toward political participation of citizens. The author concludes: "Apparently attitudes toward political activity are so strongly channeled through other agencies in

13 *Ibid.*, p. 489.
14 *Ibid.*, p. 490.

each community that the civic education program's efforts have little independent effect." [15] We suggested in a previous chapter that participation attitudes tend to be closely related to family example and training.

A study conducted in New Zealand high schools reports that the conventional social science curriculum appears to have little affect on attitudes toward national groups. However, a manipulated curriculum, in conjunction with concerted teacher effort, made a significant improvement in attitudes basic to international understanding. The author concludes: ". . . schools make little contribution to international understanding unless teachers deliberately plan to foster it." [16] Another study also reports that special types of curricula may have greater influence.[17] American students who learned about West Africans by reading only historical and geographic accounts expressed more social distance from the Africans, and a desire to maintain such distance, than did a class who read about the daily lives of the people, the problems they faced, and the help being given them through international aid bodies.

In yet another study, the authors reported that American high school students taking civics courses differ only marginally from students not enrolled in such courses.[18] At best, attending a class in American government leads to incremental increases in a student's level of political information, his sense of political effectiveness, his feeling of patriotism, or his propensity to be a political participant. This study is consistent with material presented earlier; the American high-school student is already socialized with respect to many political attributes by this stage in his life cycle. Civics courses have little influence.

15 *Ibid.*, p. 490. As we shall see below, the level of educational achievement considerably affects orientation toward political participation.

16 Warwick B. Elley, "Attitude Change and Education for International Understanding," *Sociology of Education*, XXXVII (1964), p. 325.

17 H. Murray Williams, "Changes in Pupils' Attitudes Toward West African Negroes Following the Use of Two Different Teaching Methods," *British Journal of Educational Psychology*, XXXI (1961), pp. 292–296.

18 Kenneth P. Langton and M. Kent Jennings, "Political Socialization and the High School Civics Curriculum in the United States," University of Michigan, unpublished manuscript, 1967.

However, the influence of the civics curriculum is quite different if the student is a Negro. Negroes who take civics courses do alter many of their political views. This suggests an important generalization for political socialization theory. For the white student, the material presented in a civics course is more or less redundant; he has heard it all before. For many Negro students, on the other hand, the material is new and presents them with political images and ideas that have not yet been part of their socialization experiences. The ghetto-raised Negro high school student has not had the advantages of middle class society — books, magazines, travel, family vacations to Washington, D.C., and so forth. The "newness" of the civics course makes it an important political socialization agent. For the white student, the redundancy of the course lessens its effect. These few studies linking curriculum to the formation of political orientations are more suggestive than definitive. Their findings vary. It seems clear, however, that in the absence of formal civic education, members of society would be less informed about the political world. They would have less information concerning their political structures and processes. It is doubtful, however, that basic political loyalties and attachments are substantially developed or altered through such formal civic education. If the civic training in the curriculum is inconsistent with what is learned about the political world from adults, peer groups, and other agents of political socialization, it may not be very effective.

(b) *Political indoctrination.* All school systems carry on some form of political indoctrination. The myths and legends from the past, the policies and programs of the present, and the goals and aspirations of the future are taught selectively. Consciously or not, textbooks and other teaching materials justify and rationalize political practices. The goals and means of political indoctrination through classroom materials, however, are more obvious in some nations than in others. Children in different nations receive varying doses of slanted material. Political authorities permit varying degrees of honest criticism to appear in course materials.

The Soviet Union has been identified by both popular opinion and scholars as a nation that engages in considerable political indoctrination. Frederick C. Barghoorn writes that: "The Soviet leaders seek to shape communication and personal relationships in school, family and other attitude-forming institutions so as to inculcate the maximum possible devotion to the polity." [19] The Soviet principles of pedagogy, first formulated in the 1930's, accept as their aim "the formation of behavior, character, and traits of personality necessary to the Soviet state." [20] The most important teaching agent has been the schools. Indeed, according to Jeremy Azrael, the chief goal of the educational experience has been to inculcate "loyalty and support for the polity, its leaders and their policies." [21] A major part of this indoctrination is done through the curriculum. Ideological considerations have led to the politicization of the entire curriculum, with the heaviest burden being placed on the social sciences and humanities.[22] Songbooks. readers, and textbooks have been designed to convince students that the accomplishments of the Soviet people in science and art, in agriculture and industry, are unequaled anywhere in the world.

The Soviet Union is not the only instance of extensive use of school curricula for political indoctrination. Richard Fagen has translated an arithmetic workbook used in Cuban schools for worker and peasant education which has many examples of such curriculum manipulation. One of the more suggestive problem-exercises goes like this:

> Imperialism knows no other type of relations between States except domination and subjugation, the oppression of the weak by the strong. It bases international relations on abuse and threat, on violence and arbitrariness.
>
> Between January 3 and June 10 in 1961, North American military airplanes violated Cuban airspace 3 times in the month of January, 15 in February, 17 in March, 9 in April, 8 in May, and 10 in June. What was the average monthly number of vio-

---

[19] Frederick C. Barghoorn, *Politics in the USSR* (Boston: Little, Brown, 1966), p. 84.

[20] Quoted by Barghoorn, *ibid.*, p. 85, from N. A. Lyalin (ed.), *Kollektiv i razvitie lichnosti shkolnika* (Leningrad, 1962), p. 28.

[21] Jeremy R. Azrael, "Soviet Union," in Coleman, *op. cit.*, p. 237.

[22] *Ibid.*, p. 238.

lations of Cuban air space by North American military airplanes? [23]

A South African textbook in a subject called "Race Relations" includes the following:

> Our forefathers believed, and we still believe today, that God himself made the diversity of peoples on earth. . . . Inter-racial residence and inter-marriage are not only a disgrace, but also forbidden by law. It is, however, not only the skin of the South African that differs from that of the nonwhite. The white stands on a much higher plane of civilization and is more developed. Whites must so live, learn and work that we shall not sink to the cultural level of the nonwhites. Only thus can the government of our country remain in the hands of the whites.[24]

The kibbutz experiments in Israeli education afford another example of how a curriculum can be permeated by a national ideology. In his study of child training on a kibbutz, Melford Spiro quotes a paragraph from a statement describing the educational philosophy:

> The aims which express our *weltanschauung* should be expressed in every study-project, in every discussion, and in every socio-cultural activity. In every subject — nature, the Homeland, Bible, economics — one should uncover the political causes that are concealed in these subjects: criticism of society, social justice, existence of social classes, national oppression, exile and suffering of Jews. . . .

From his observations of classroom discussions, Spiro concludes that many discussions are "ideological indoctrination which are labeled . . . as scientific truth rather than ideology." [25]

In one context or another all nations indulge in some form of political indoctrination through textbooks and classroom materials. The existence of such efforts can be easily doc-

[23] Richard R. Fagen, *Cuba: The Political Content of Adult Education* (Stanford: The Hoover Institution of War and Peace, 1964), p. 68.

[24] Leonard M. Thompson, *Politics in the Republic of South Africa* (Boston: Little, Brown, 1966), p. 100.

[25] Melford E. Spiro, *Children of the Kibbutz* (New York: Schocken Books, 1965), p. 257.

umented. However, knowing that a school's curriculum includes a certain type of lesson tells us little about its influence.
The articulation of a particular value in a classroom is not
presumptive evidence that the value is internalized by the
student. Students rarely become perfect replicas of the model
citizen portrayed in such political indoctrination. In some
instances political indoctrination efforts in the classroom,
like some attempts as civic education, may be quite ineffective.

Azrael, in his analysis of Soviet education, points out short-
comings of a political indoctrination program. Among other
unintended consequences, crude political indoctrination in
the Soviet Union appears to bore the students. Soviet students
become politically apathetic, "from sheer overwhelming bore-
dom aroused by the dogmatism and repetitiveness of all political communication sponsored by the regime, whether in the
classroom, the Komsomol, or the mass media." [26]

Although it is not always successful in meeting the regime's
objectives, the classroom curriculum stands as a key means
through which school children acquire knowledge about political life and loyalty to the nation. As more of the population
of the world comes to spend an increasingly larger portion of
their formative years in classrooms, we can expect the curriculum to assume increasing importance in political socialization.

2. *Classroom Ritual Life.* Political values are also transmitted to the child through the ritual life of the classroom —
saluting the flag, singing patriotic songs, honoring national
heroes and events, and being exposed to patriotic symbols
such as pictures and sayings of leaders. With greater or lesser
self-consciousness, schools throughout the world append to
the normal curriculum numerous ceremonial expressions of
devotion to the nation. Educational policy makers assume that
systematic exposure to such symbols will produce greater attachment and respect to the nation and its institutions. Patriotic feelings are formed and cemented by participation in
ritual acts.

A major indicator of the importance placed on ritual exercises is the amount of time and resources allocated to them. Teachers are compelled, by social norms if not always by law, to spend valuable school hours and scarce resources on classroom activities and programs which stress national patriotism. Such investments are made in the overextended school systems of developing nations as well as in more affluent countries. A recent parliamentary debate on educational policy in an African country concluded that copies of the national anthem should be printed and distributed to every school in the nation, including schools suffering from such critical disadvantages as no electricity and no writing materials.

A particularly rich illustration of the ritual life of the school is presented in Herbert Passin's discussion of Imperial Japan.[27] He writes that the official doctrine of the state was promoted in a variety of ways, not the least of which was the ritual activity expected of every student.

> There were frequent ceremonial assemblies requiring the reading of the Imperial Rescript on Education, the showing of the Imperial Portraits, the raising of the national flag, etc., and these were carried through with the utmost protocol and graveness to make a proper impression on the children. . . . So sacred were these symbols that in case of fire they were to be saved before everything else, even at the risk of life. . . . The cult of the state . . . was brought into close relation with the school system. Its doctrines were taught, and pupils were required to participate in its rituals and visit its shrines on ceremonial and national occasions. Schools organized pilgrimages and outings designed to strengthen the pupils' loyalty and devotion to the national cult.[28]

The fact that ritual experiences are stressed in the classroom and that they are deemed an important part of political indoc-

[27] Passin describes in some detail the indoctrination efforts of Japanese educational authorities. Like Azrael, he questions the effect of the political indoctrination campaigns. "It is clear . . . that there were strong elements of resistance to the penetration of the official doctrine. . . . Nor is there any evidence that the officially promoted morality penetrated as deeply among the masses as the leaders might have hoped. For many people, the official dogmas were mere formalities external to themselves and their way of life." See his "Japan" in Coleman, *ibid.*, pp. 310–311.

[28] *Ibid.*, pp. 308–309.

trination programs by most regimes, however, does not give a clear picture of what is contained in them, how effective they are, and how important they are in relation to other socialization methods. A clear statement on these issues must await much more research. We can, however, suggest two possible implications of the students' ritual life.

(a) In one sense rituals are the acting out of one's sense of awe toward what is symbolized by the ritual. Basic feelings of patriotism and loyalty are reinforced as one acts out his devotion to the state. In their report on American school children, Hess and Torney comment:

The feelings of respect for the pledge and the national anthem are reinforced daily and are seldom questioned by the child.[29]

The authors continue by pointing out that the very gestures and words associated with the acts suggest submission, respect, and dependence. They conclude that the rituals "establish an emotional orientation toward country and flag even though an understanding of the meaning of the words and actions has not been developed. These seem to be indoctrinating acts that cue and reinforce feelings of loyalty and patriotism." [30]

In some instances these ritual experiences in school may reinforce political loyalties that have already been formed in the family; in others they may introduce the child to such orientations. The former pattern is likely to occur in more established polities, and the latter may be a significant phenomenon in newer nations. Either way, such ritual experiences are of great importance. "This early orientation prepares the child for later learning and stresses the importance of loyalty for citizens of all ages." [31]

(b) *Rituals also emphasize the collective nature of patriotism.* Saluting the flag, singing the anthems, and honoring national figures are group activities. Group experiences can be very compelling, especially to the impressionable mind of the child. Consider the difference between the classroom and

29 Robert D. Hess and Judith V. Torney, *The Development of Political Attitudes in Children* (Chicago: Aldine Publishing Co., 1967), p. 106.
30 *Ibid.*
31 *Ibid.*, p. 108.

the family as settings for acquiring emotional attachment to the country. In the family, the child may learn to be patriotic because he recognizes that this orientation is highly valued by adults he tries to imitate. Patriotism in the classroom, in contrast, is *acted out* in the rituals, and acted out by the individual in a group he has come to be closely related with. In an attenuated way, the classroom approximates the "we-feeling" that is an important part of the political culture. The rituals lay the groundwork for adult political activity — most of which is necessarily group activity. Nationalism, partisanship, and identification with a social or political movement are orientations more meaningful when experienced as part of a collectivity. The ritual life of the school often involves such collective experiences.

3. *The Teacher.* The third way in which the classroom affects political socialization is through the teacher. Because of the special role he has in society and the direct contact he has with youth during the formative years, the teacher has considerable influence on the child's political orientations.

First, for the child the teacher represents an authoritative spokesman of society. The teacher is often the first model of political authority the beginning student encounters. How new this kind of authority is to a child can be seen by comparing the parent and the teacher. When a child responds to his parent as an authority figure, he does not separate the role from the incumbent of the role. He keeps the same parent permanently. Consequently, parents are very personal authority figures; they dispense rewards and punishments in what often appear to be idiosyncratic and even capricious ways. The public school teacher as an authority figure, on the other hand, is much more like a political authority. The child learns that the authority role and incumbent of the role are separate factors. He learns he should obey any incumbent who happens to occupy the role "teacher." Further, he discovers that rewards and punishments from authorities are affected by identifiable constraints that operate on the particular person in the role. The teacher, like the policeman, president, or mayor, is part of an institutional pattern, a constitutional order.

In addition to his position of authority in the classroom, the teacher also benefits from a position of general respect and trust in his community. Especially in rural areas and villages, people look up to the public school teacher as a repository of knowledge and civilization. In some locations he also enjoys prestige as the major representative of the government. In African villages the teacher is presumptively a community leader in activities ranging far beyond education. The East African political socialization study cited previously found that eight of ten students reported they could always or almost always trust their teachers. The teacher stands on a par with parents and religious leaders as a recipient of widespread good-will.[32]

The teacher serves as society's representative and partner in the task of rearing children; he is generally respected and is expected to be a model of behavior and of social values. The more important issue here, however, is how and to what degree the teacher affects the political development of his charges. We can inquire into these questions in two ways: (1) The teacher as a holder of specific political values and opinions and a disseminator of such orientations; and, (2) the teacher as creator and manipulator of a "learning culture" in the classroom, which has important indirect political consequences.

(a) *The teacher as disseminator of political values*. The evidence about the public school teacher in the United States forms a consistent picture. Teachers are expected to, and do,

[32] East African Education and Citizenship Project. This study is being carried out under the auspices of the East African Institute of Social Research. Investigators include David Koff, George Von der Muhll, and Kenneth Prewitt. Reports of the data are based on the pretest or on samples from the data. Preliminary papers prepared thus far include: Koff and Von der Muhll, "Political Socialization in Kenya and Tanzania — A Comparative Analysis," *Journal of Modern African Studies*, Vol. 5, #1 (1967); Koff, "Education and Employment Perspectives of Kenya Primary Pupils," in James Sheffield (ed), *Education, Employment and Rural Development* (Nairobi: East African Publishing House, 1967); Prewitt, "Political Education and Political Socialization," in Roberta Sigel (ed.), *Learning about Politics — Studies in Political Socialization* (New York: Random House, forthcoming). Relevant essays have been collected in Prewitt (ed.), *Education and Political Values: Essays about East Africa* (Nairobi: East African Publishing House, 1969).

propagate political views and beliefs appropriately labeled "consensus values." Teachers should not, and generally do not, use the classroom as a forum for discussion of "partisan values" and controversial positions. Democracy, the two-party system, free enterprise, basic freedoms, and so forth, are not only permissible subjects in the classroom; the teacher is expected to urge these beliefs on his students. Liberal or conservative positions, foreign policy views, party allegiances, on the other hand, are seen as partisan values; and the teacher generally is expected to avoid particular interpretations of such issues.

The teacher, then, is expected simultaneously to be very political in some senses, and apolitical in others. The evidence suggests that the American public school teacher is generally adroit in balancing these two demands. A similar state exists among public school teachers throughout the world.[33] A polity cannot afford to have its school system rent by partisan debates; but neither can it afford a public education system negligent in transmitting the basic political norms of the society. This is the general pattern for public school systems. The picture may be quite different for some private and parochial schools. In such schools one of the major objectives may be to inculcate particular partisan or group values, some of which might be at odds with the general consensus values of the larger society.[34]

The teacher's role as conveyer of consensus values is so widely assumed that few students of political socialization have investigated it. One major reason why teachers operate so effectively in this connection is that they are products of

[33] Carl H. Lande, for instance, writes of the public school teacher in the Philippines that "The civic role played by school teachers has been affected by their status as public employees. Like other civil servants, public school teachers are supposed to eschew partisan politics." See his "Philippines," in Coleman, *op. cit.*, p. 338.

[34] This is particularly well illustrated in a study of the political socialization of Mennonite youth. Students of a Mennonite school, for instance, rank the armed forces as the thing they are least proud of in the United States (from a list of ten items). Two control groups from "average American high schools" ranked this item first. See Daniel R. Leatherman, "The Political Socialization of Students in the Mennonite Secondary Schools," unpublished M.A. thesis, University of Chicago, 1960.

the same political socialization for which they serve as agents. Teachers generally do not need to be taught to laud the virtues of the nation. Their own political selves have been shaped in accordance with the very consensus values they now transmit. This condition is more prevalent in older, established nations than in newer, developing ones. In the latter teachers are frequently sent through accelerated courses designed to teach them the new "consensus values."

The extent to which consensus and patriotic values are part of the orientations of American school teachers is indicated in a survey of high school teachers. Forty-two per cent of the teachers sampled considered the following statement to be fact rather than opinion: "The American form of government may not be perfect, but it is the best type of government yet devised by man." All but 3 per cent of these teachers, whether they considered the statement fact or opinion, felt it was a view which could be freely expressed in the classroom.[35]

A study on "Citizenship and Education in East Africa" testifies to the importance of the teacher and the schools in teaching citizenship in these new nations. When asked who had taught them the most about being a good citizen of their country — parents and relatives, political leaders, religious leaders, or teachers — primary and secondary students in Kenya, Tanzania, and Uganda overwhelmingly chose their teachers. Table IX.2 presents additional findings from this study, showing the importance the students assign to citizenship training as a function of the school. East African students appear to trust their teachers, think that they are the most important sources of instruction about citizenship, and think that the teaching of citizenship is the most important purpose for a school.[36]

We conclude this section with an observation Hess and Torney made after reporting on extensive data comparing teachers' views and students' attitudes. They find that teachers and students are more alike in their attitudes in areas where

---

[35] Harmon Zeigler, *The Political World of the High School Teacher* (Eugene, Ore.: The Center for the Advanced Study of Educational Administration, University of Oregon, 1966), p. 130.

[36] *Ibid.;* see, in particular, Koff and Van der Muhll.

TABLE IX.2   *Rank Order of Purposes a School Might Have:*
            East African Secondary School Students

Purposes	Kenya	Tanzania	Uganda
Teach students to be good citizens of	1	1	1
Teach students the skills necessary to get jobs	2	2	3
Teach students the important things to know for the exams	3	3	2
Teach students to be religious (to be good Christians, etc.)	4	4	4
Teach students about the important African traditions and customs	5	5	5

Source: East African Education and Citizenship Project, unpublished paper.

there is consensus in the society (*e.g.,* the behavior of the good citizen) and less similar in attitudes which lack such consensus (political parties).[37] This finding offers strong support for the ideas we have developed in this section. Teachers communicate to their students the political consensus values of society. They appear to have some influence. Teachers do not talk as often about partisan values. There is more discrepancy between teacher and student and among the students on these issues. Partisan or group values are acquired elsewhere and generally are not affected by the school classroom.

(b) *The teacher and the learning culture.* The teacher also affects the political development of the student by establishing some sort of "learning culture" or "social system" in the classroom. The elementary school teacher with whom millions of children the world over have daily contact is institutionally defined as superior to the child. He knows more about the subject matter, establishes and interprets school rules, is looked up to as a behavioral model, and is publicly labeled a representative of society's authority over the young. In a normal day the elementary teacher will have more than 10,000 exchanges with the student through which he will transmit numerous cultural values. Some of these values, as discussed above, will have specific political content; others will have latent political

[37] Hess and Torney, *op. cit.,* pp. 110–115.

meaning. As the first person to represent to the child the large, impersonal society beyond the personal family circle, the elementary teacher cannot avoid influencing the impressionable child in ways beyond the formal curriculum. We can illustrate this in two areas of politically relevant learning: obedience and competitiveness.

In a French village school, four- and five-year-olds are started in the *classes enfantines*. A teacher responsible for these young charges reports: "There is nothing serious that they have to learn for a year or so." Wylie, studying the village school, thinks differently: "The four-year-old and five-year-old children, however, *do* learn important lessons. They learn to sit still for long periods. They learn to accept the discipline of the school. . . . They are not encouraged to 'express their personality.' On the contrary they learn that their personality must be kept constantly under control." [38] Wylie's observation probably applies to most school systems. The lesson of obedience is learned early and is very important for political and social life.

Evidence from American elementary school children links the "lesson of obedience" more closely with political learning. Elementary teachers place more emphasis on compliance to rules and authority than any other "political" topic. Second and third grade teachers consider the obligation of the child to conform to school rules and laws of the community a more important lesson than reading and arithmetic. This concern with compliance appears to be characteristic of teachers of all elementary grades.[39] At the same time that teachers emphasize compliance, they underemphasize the right of citizens to participate in government. Hess and Torney conclude that "much of what is called citizenship training in the public schools does not teach the child about the city, state, or national government, but is an attempt to teach regard for the rules and standards of conduct of the school." [40]

Competitiveness is another politically meaningful orienta-

[38] Wylie, *op. cit.*, p. 57.
[39] Hess and Torney, *op. cit.*, p. 110.
[40] *Ibid.*, p. 218.

tion learned in the classroom. The authors of a leading text-book on education in the United States write: "The child learns that it is serious to fail, important to succeed, that the society disapproves of slow people and rewards fast ones." [41] A simple fourth grade spelling contest conveys this lesson. Whether the student masters the intricacies of spelling or not, he internalizes the cultural value of competitiveness and success.

A comparison of the "lesson in competitiveness" learned by the American fourth grader with that taught to the Israeli fourth grader in the kibbutz is instructive. The philosophy of kibbutz education is to minimize competition among students. Students are not graded. No competitive rating system is used to reward or punish. Students cannot fail; all are promoted at the end of the year. The cultural value of equality, it is thought, would be compromised if schools rewarded performance differentially.[42] The kibbutz pattern is interesting primarily as a deviation. Most schools attempt to elicit performance by comparing one student with another.

In an article entitled "The School Class as a Social System," Parsons enlarges on the notion of the learning culture as a socialization experience.[43] He points out that the child enters school with only one social role clearly determined, that of being a boy or a girl. Beyond that, the child is free to choose among the available roles. He can be a worker or a player; he can be a leader or a follower; he can be well behaved or a problem child; he can be a success or a failure, and so on. His status as the son in his family is fixed by his biological characteristics; his status in the classroom social system will be fixed by how he performs valued tasks. His status is achieved rather than ascribed. In this regard the classroom as a social system reflects the larger social and political systems more than does the family. At least in American society, the expectation is that a person gets what he deserves. His rights are an equal

---

[41] Robert J, Havighurst and Bernice L. Neugarten, *Society and Education* (Boston: Allyn & Bacon, 1957), p. 508.

[42] For an extended discussion of this point see Spiro, *op. cit.*, pp. 258–264.

[43] *Harvard Educational Review*, XXIV (1959), pp. 297–318.

chance and the rewards of his efforts. In Parson's words, "There is thus a basic sense in which the elementary school class is an embodiment of the fundamental American value of equality of opportunity, in that it places value *both* on initial equality and on differential achievement." [44]

The basic point here is that attitudes toward achievement, toward change, toward fair play, toward manipulability of the environment, toward cooperation, as well as toward obedience and competitiveness, can be shaped by the culture of the classroom. As we stressed in Chapter V, such components of one's world have important "spill-over" effects and shape political outlooks.

The amount of harmony between the values shaped in the classroom and those applicable to the political world do vary, of course. A lack of harmony is noticeable in certain new nations of the world. In East Africa there is today considerable discrepancy between the school culture and the national ideology. While the political leaders stress egalitarian democracy, the schools are run by an elitist, hierarchic prefectorial system. While the political leaders stress African socialism, the classrooms remain wedded to the norm of individual achievement. The values implicitly transmitted by the school as a social system are incongruent with the articulated national aspirations. [45]

With these examples and notions in mind, we can turn to the aspect of the teacher's role in the classroom considered most important to political socialization: the authoritarian or democratic atmosphere of the classroom. Classrooms are said to be more or less democratic (or authoritarian) depending on how the teacher handles his role as authority figure. He may stress disciplined learning of the material presented, rigid adherence to rules, and a deferential attitude toward himself as the authority. Student participation may be kept to a minimum. Or, the teacher may assume an opposite stance. More student participation may be encouraged. School rules may be

---

[44] *Ibid.*, p. 309.
[45] This point is reviewed in Prewitt, "Political Education and Political Socialization," *loc. cit.*

few and relaxed. The teacher may require less deference from students.

The crucial notion for political socialization is that these conditions affect the political outlook of the students. Democratic leadership by the teacher fosters attitudes and skills consonant with democratic values. The authoritarian teacher induces his charges to think according to hierarchy and deference to power. This notion has two variants: One line of reasoning stresses the teacher as a role model, the other concerns the importance of student participation for learning.

Postwar Germany provides an interesting example of the application of this proposition about classroom atmosphere. Both the occupation forces after the war and the new German government were concerned with remaking Germany into a democracy. Education was to be the key to this transformation. Curriculum reform was considered only a part of the effort needed. Attention was focused also on the method of instruction and the social atmosphere of the schools. "The classroom was to be more democratic, and student participation in the administration of school was to be fostered." [46] It is too early to evaluate the success of this program, but it is interesting that 38 per cent of German students who were 12 between 1946 and 1953, and only 6 per cent who were 12 between 1941 and 1945 reported actual participation in school discussions and debates.[47] These data suggest that alterations in the classroom atmosphere are possible. Whether such alterations can have the desired political effect cannot yet be ascertained.

Some of the findings of the five-nation study by Almond and Verba are suggestive here, however. The authors find considerable variation among countries in the rate of student participation allowed in the classroom. The ranking of the five countries from high to low in the "democratic" atmosphere of the classroom is: (1) the United States, (2) Great Britain, (3) Germany, (4) Italy, and (5) Mexico. This ranking cor-

[46] Sidney Verba, "Germany: The Remaking of Political Culture," in Pye and Verba (eds.), *Political Culture and Political Development* (Princeton: Princeton University Press, 1965), p. 161.

[47] These data are computed from a table presented in Almond and Verba, *The Civic Culture* (Princeton: Princeton University Press, 1963), p. 339.

responds to the extent of democracy in each of the five nations, according to measures devised by Almond and Verba. In addition, persons within each nation who recalled being able to participate in the classroom turned out to be more politically competent than those presumably unable to participate.[48]

4. *Summary.* We have now reviewed three ways in which the formal classroom and educational program serve as political socialization agents: the curriculum, the ritual life, and the teacher. It should be quite apparent that the school molds political characteristics in both direct and indirect ways. The classroom in a number of different ways serves as a very important agent of political learning, one that is often employed consciously and deliberately by society's leaders to assure political support and knowledge. We now turn to some of the less formal aspects which affect the process of political maturation.

NONCLASSROOM FORMS

1. *The Social Composition of the School.* Educational theorists and cultural engineers have long sought to use the social composition of schools for the specific purposes of influencing political orientations. The social class, ethnic, racial, tribal, and religious makeup of the student and staff population of a school are assumed to influence the views students have toward social groupings in society at large. In the United States, the mass public school system has long been accepted and promoted as a contributor to intergroup equality and cooperation. The traditional class-based schools of Britain, on the other hand, have contributed to a more socially stratified culture and a system in which leadership has been drawn largely from the upper classes.

The current controversy in American cities over bussing students from diversified areas of a city to mixed schools in order to assure racial and socially integrated classrooms illustrates well the importance placed on the social composition of the schools. Both opponents and proponents of bussing base their arguments on the premise that the composition of the

[48] Almond and Verba, *op. cit.,* pp. 352–363.

student body has consequences for social and political learning. The proponents argue that students from various social class and racial backgrounds should be brought together in common facilities to counteract residential segregation, to promote multigroup understanding, and to avoid teaching racial discrimination. An argument advanced by opponents of bussing is that neighborhood schools should be preserved to maintain neighborhood identification, activity, and cooperation. Each neighborhood should have its own exclusive school with which it identifies.

Although the goals of these positions are at odds, they share a common socialization proposition. A person's contacts with other individuals affect his way of viewing the social and political world. The composition of a student body can aid in the development of community identification or prevent it. It can help create intergroup cooperation and harmony, or isolation and conflict. Of the many social institutions the child knows, the school is most important in this regard. The school is the first major institution most children have experience with outside the limited and protective shell of the family. When the child enters the formal educational system, he is confronted with a larger and more diversified population of peers and authority figures than he experienced in the home or in the smaller, neighborhood peer groups. From these new contacts the young child learns about articulating and solving collective problems, about asserting and protecting rights in competition with others, and about the possibilities of social cooperation or conflict.

Whether the school population is socially homogeneous or whether it more accurately reflects the heterogeneity of the adult world will affect social adjustment patterns. In particular, the child's development of stereotypes and prejudices is influenced by the makeup of the school population. In Chapter II we pointed out that a basic component of the political self is a set of social categories, identifications, and prejudices through which to filter political happenings. The development of these filters is significantly influenced by the social composition of this first major nonfamily group. In many instances the school, which tries to promote social integration and toleration through a socially diversified student body, is working directly against the socialization of the more particularistic family. Family training is often geared toward a more exclusive social outlook, toward differentiating family members from other groups of people.

Most of the specific attention to social composition has been directed toward its effect upon prejudice and discrimination. Contact with diversified types of people is assumed to facilitate understanding and cooperation between groups. Studies of the actual results of such integration have yielded mixed findings. On balance, however, most observers feel that increased contact between various groupings in society aids in the creation of a political order in which cooperation among groups replaces patterns of discrimination and hostility. A segregated society and a segregated school system heighten the tendency toward rigid and inaccurate stereotyping. As one student of race relations has put it: "Prejudices are generally acquired slowly and over a period of time. The child acquires his ethnic values and racial attitudes as he learns other social lessons from adults, from his peers, and from his life experiences. Groups that are segregated in schools or in the community he assumes are inferior because society treats them as inferiors." [49] This probability was recognized in the famous 1954 Supreme Court decision on public school segregation. The Court held that the maintenance of segregated schools institutionalized cultural patterns of prejudice, and caused whites and blacks to share a set of values contributing to barriers between them.

We have emphasized the manipulation of the school composition as a means of increasing cooperation and understanding. Of course, many societies compose their schools for the opposite reason. In some instances, as in South Africa, this is the intention of a national educational plan. More often, however, group differentiation is promoted by special subgroup schools. Numerous subgroups in society (racial, religious, ethnic, and social class) seek to promote group values and to differentiate

[49] M. Vosk, "Correlates of Prejudice," *Review of Educational Research*, XXIII (1953), pp. 353–361. Quoted in Bernard Berelson and Gary A. Steiner, *Human Behavior* (New York: Harcourt, Brace & World, 1964), p. 507.

themselves specifically from the rest of society. They establish their own school systems primarily to keep their members from close contact with other groups in the society. By limiting the social diversity of their schools and keeping their children out of more socially integrated public schools, particular in-group feelings and parochial loyalties can be promoted. The basic goal in this instance is different from the general goal of social integration, but the same major socialization variable is at work.

2. *Extracurricular Activities and Student Political Groups*. In addition to their formal academic programs most schools maintain extracurricular activities and groups. The number of such activities varies greatly from culture to culture. Their proliferation is most extensive in the United States, where the academic program of the average school is supplemented by dozens of clubs, performing groups, student governments, and athletic activities. These activities help to provide the student with skills appropriate for his integration into the pluralistic adult political world.

We cannot begin to chronicle here the variety of organizations and experiences available to the contemporary student. We can, however, make distinctions between two forms of groups. There are, first, numerous groups concerned with school affairs or occupational preparation — *e.g.*, student government, music and dramatic groups, and sports. In addition, many schools have, either officially or unofficially, connections with specifically political organizations. In some instances, such as the Young Pioneers in the Soviet Union and the Hitler Youth in Nazi Germany, they are regulated and sponsored by the government. In others they are sponsored by political parties or other partisan groups. In the United States branches of the Young Republicans and Young Democrats, Students for a Democratic Society, and various civil rights and peace groups are more specifically political organizations. Both types of organization have consequences for citizenship and political training, but their influence is different.

(a) *School-based activities*. Those activities specifically tied in with the school are relevant as political socialization agents because they train the student for political participation and teach him the cultural values associated with it. At least extra-curricular activities have been promoted by school officials for just these reasons. One observer comments on their utility as follows:

> The extracurricular activity was given an important position in the philosophy of the democratic school. High school extra-curricular activities were to be analogous to adult voluntary associations. Just as a membership in a voluntary association was believed to have positive effects on an adult's citizenship competence, so would the extracurricular activity have positive effects on the teenager. Participation would give him insight and awareness into social processes. He would acquire an ability to manipulate these processes. He would have a greater under-standing of how things get done in the larger political system. He would have a more positive orientation toward political phenomena. So the argument went.[50]

The consequences of these activities are varied. The sports pro-grams of the schools may teach the student the culturally pre-scribed values of competition and sportsmanship. In American society the student is taught to compete, to seek to win, but to do so within the proper "rules of the game." He is also taught to lose with good grace. Such norms are, of course, generally appropriate for broad aspects of adult social life. In other cul-tures the appropriate values of the society are also learned through the procedures surrounding various sports.

The activity with the greatest direct relevance for political learning is student government. Student governments are set up, by and large, to teach the student the values of self-govern-ment and to familiarize him with the forms and procedures he will face in the adult political world. For a minority of stu-dents, student governments also provide direct experiences in governmental positions, which are generally designed in form and title as prototypes of the governmental institutions of the adult political world.

As with other aspects of school life, it is difficult to assess the effect of extracurricular activities. Research on these relation-

---

[50] David Ziblatt, "High School Extracurricular Activities and Political Socialization," in *The Annals of the American Academy of Political and Social Science,* CCCLXI (September 1965), p. 23.

ships is not extensive. Two studies of American high schools offer limited and mixed findings on how participation in extracurricular activities affects attitudes toward politics. One study found positive relationships between the degree of participation in extracurricular activities in a high school and responses suggesting a sense of political efficacy, an appreciation of political parties, a feeling of the legitimacy of political institutions, and the expectation of future political participation.[51] Another study failed to find direct correlations between participation and attitudes toward politics; but found rather that a feeling of integration into the high school social status system was associated with social trust. "It is this social trust and not the direct experience of extracurricular participation which is linked with a positive attitude toward politics." [52]

These limited studies provide only partial answers to the question of how extracurricular activities affect political socialization. It might be productive to compare schools having extensive extracurricular activities with schools more impoverished in this regard. That is, it may not be rates of individual involvement which affect political orientations so much as the general school culture. Inactive students in a school with a rich extracurricular life will have their views shaped by the generally accepted participatory norms. A research design comparing schools rather than individuals within a single school could clear up ambiguities reflected in the studies cited above.

(b) *Student political groups and activities.* A minority of students get involved in student political organizations as part of their school experiences. Such experiences strongly affect the political learning of those involved. The students, in these instances, are a special case of a general socialization phenomenon referred to throughout our discussion. A person's direct experiences with the political world help to shape his political self. Through his involvement in political demonstrations, movements, and organizations the student comes into

51 Helen Sonnenburg Lewis, "The Teen-age Joiner and his Orientation Toward Public Affairs: A Test of Two Multiple Group Membership Hypotheses" (unpublished Ph.D. dissertation, Department of Political Science, Michigan State University, 1962), quoted in Ziblatt, *ibid.*, p. 24.

52 Ziblatt, *op. cit.*, p. 31.

direct contact with the political world. This encounter has considerable consequences for the development of his political orientations. As one commentator has put it, student organizations concerned with politics "are usually the main source of political education for the students involved in them, and often have a vital and lasting effect on those involved." [53]

The amount of political participation and involvement in student political organizations varies from nation to nation, but nowhere does it involve more than a small minority of the student body. The popular picture of a whole student body participating in riots and demonstrations is a distorted one for the college and university populations of the developing countries, as well as for those of more developed nations.[54] Lipset estimates that the combined membership of the junior affiliates of United States political parties constitute about 2 per cent of the total student population.[55]

The amount, form, and direction of student participation in politics differs greatly from nation to nation, and from one generation to another. In Latin American countries university students have traditionally been forces in national politics, and students are politically active in greater proportions than are students in North America. Asian and African students have played critical roles in their independence movements and continue to play active parts in national politics. Some generations of students seem more prone to political involvement than others. In the United States, the 1930's was a period of student interest and participation. The late 1940's and 1950's are generally regarded as a period of student political apathy. The mid-1960's have witnessed a period of renewed political interest; students are participating in the civil rights move-

[53] Philip G. Altbach, "Students and Politics," *Comparative Education Review*, X (1966), p. 185. This issue of the *Comparative Education Review*, edited by S. M. Lipset, is devoted to student politics. Many of the ideas of this section are drawn from this volume.

[54] Claucio A. D. Soares, "The Active Few: Student Ideology and Participation in Developing Countries," *ibid.*, p. 205.

[55] Quoted in S. M. Lipset and Philip G. Altbach, "Student Politics and Higher Education in the United States," *ibid.*, p. 320. For a general discussion of the Berkeley revolt, see S. M. Lipset and Sheldon S. Wolin (eds.), *The Berkeley Student Revolt: Facts and Interpretations* (New York: Doubleday, 1965).

ment, the peace movement, in programs designed to help underprivileged elements of the population, and in attempts to democratize the schools. In other nations other factors have been the cause of student political involvement. In France, the war years and involvement in the resistance continue to influence contemporary student politics. Colonial control gave rise to student demonstrations in India, Algeria, and numerous other colonial areas after World War II and up through the mid-1960's. Disaffection with national policies and administrations have mobilized student activists in Turkey, Korea, South Vietnam, Spain, and the Sudan.

The forms, causes, and results of student political participation form a complex picture. There seem to be at least a few general patterns, however. *First,* student political involvement tends to radicalize political orientations. Whatever political views a student has, leftist or rightist, they tend to be intensified and radicalized in the crucible of student politics. Several factors account for this. The student is "acting out" his political views in a highly emotional situation, as part of a collective which gives him support and feeds his political commitments. The student frequently feels shut out of normal avenues of political expression. He is too young to vote and often ignored by his elders. He generally has fewer direct responsibilities in his society and thus has fewer restraints.

Second, although both right and left oriented students are radicalized through involvement, students of liberal orientations are more likely to become engaged in student movements than are their conservative classmates. This bias results from the fact that left-leaning students tend more than rightists to view studenthood as part of, rather than preliminary to, an adult citizen role.[56] It also stems from the general tendency for colleges to be more congenial to liberally oriented student groups than to conservative ones.

Third, though only a small minority of the student population are activists, student movements influence a much larger part of the student population. Nonactivist sympathizers as well as student onlookers find themselves altering political

[56] This is an argument presented by Soares, *op. cit.,* p. 206.

views in accord with the opinion leadership provided by the activists. The activists often define or redefine political issues in such a way that all segments of the student body will respond and thus reformulate political outlooks.

For a small number of participants, political groups serve as recruiting agencies for adult political roles. Many political organizations sponsor student groups as a means of finding future leaders for their own organizations. Likewise some students, already set on political careers, use student political groups as stepping stones for adult political aspirations. In either case student political organizations are probably important sources of experience, for future political leaders and participants.

EDUCATION AND POLITICAL ORIENTATIONS

Thus far we have discussed how the school serves as an agent of political socialization. In this section we discuss the actual status of being educated as it affects political orientations. Numerous surveys demonstrate that well educated persons differ politically from less well educated persons in many important respects. The literature supporting this contention is so voluminous and well known that an extensive analysis is unnecessary. Level of education, either as an indicator of other social characteristics or as an attribute in its own right is universally correlated with many aspects of the political self.

V. O. Key has summarized American research findings bearing on how education affects political outlooks.[57] He spells out four dimensions of the citizen's role that are influenced by level of education: (a) Better educated persons feel a stronger sense of duty to participate in the political life of the nation than do less well educated persons. (b) The educated citizen feels a greater sense of political efficacy. He is more apt to feel that he can influence the political process, that governmental officials have regard for him and his views, and that channels of access to political power are open to him. (c) The better educated citizen is the more involved he will be in political matters. He will be more interested in politics than

[57] Key, *op. cit.*, pp. 323–331.

will the less well educated citizen. (d) Finally, education is strongly related to the probability that the citizen will be politically active. The better educated vote at a greater rate. They are also likely to engage in more demanding types of political participation such as campaigning, working for a political party, contributing money, etc.

Cross-national studies have reported similar findings. Almond and Verba, for instance, note nine major ways in which the educated in the five nations they studied differ substantially from the less well educated: [58]

1. The more educated person is more aware of the impact of government on the individual than is the person of less education.

2. The more educated individual is more likely to report that he follows politics and pays attention to election campaigns than is the individual of less education.

3. The more educated individual has more political information.

4. The more educated individual has opinions on a wider range of political subjects; the focus of his attention to politics is wider.

5. The more educated individual is more likely to engage in political discussion.

6. The more educated individual feels free to discuss politics with a wider range of people. Those with less education are more likely to report that there are many people with whom they avoid such discussions.

7. The more educated individual is more likely to consider himself capable of influencing the government; that is reflected both in responses to questions on what one could do about an unjust law and in respondent's scores on the subjective competence scale.

8. The more educated individual is more likely to be a member — an active member — of some organizations.

9. The more educated individual is more likely to express confidence in his social environment: to believe that other people are trustworthy and helpful.

There is little question that the level of education affects a citizen's perception of the political world and his relation-

[58] Almond and Verba, *op. cit.*, pp. 380–381.

ships with it. This form of influence operates in addition to the more direct effect of the schools as agents of political learning. In the bulk of this chapter we have considered how the schools provide the student with direct political education and with experiences which have latent consequences for political orientations. Here we are suggesting that "being educated" itself affects such matters as political knowledge, involvement, and sense of political ability and efficacy.

The factors causing this strong relationship between level of education and key political orientations are many and complex. We can offer four explanatory hypotheses as an initial step in explaining the relationships. An additional word of caution is needed before we proceed, however. One difficulty in assessing the influence of education on political attitudes, is that the level of education is very closely related to a number of other socioeconomic attributes — especially to income, occupation, and social class. These other factors are strongly related to political orientations. (See the discussion in Chapter X.) For that reason it is difficult to isolate the independent effect of education. In the points which follow we make no pretense at successful control of these other factors.

1. Better educated persons are involved in society's communication network. Their reading habits, travel experiences, friendship patterns, and leisure activities increase the amount of politically pertinent information available to them. Education is a skill which helps a person to act out this information, as well.

2. Citizens of higher educational status are accustomed to collective decision making. The educated are active participants in the organizational life of society. Through his social involvement, the educated person acquires habits and skills which are easily transferred to political affairs.

3. The educated citizen also acquires attitudes which are transferred to the political sphere. A clear illustration of this is the feeling of political competence. The educated tend to believe that rational manipulation of social institutions can produce desired goals. This sense of mastery and control over the social environment is generalized to politics, and the educated feel more politically efficacious than the uneducated.

4. Educated persons, because of their higher social and economic status, usually feel a greater stake in society. More than the uneducated, they presume that political events directly affect their personal well-being. The more active role taken in politics by the better educated stems, in part, from a desire to protect their investments.

This attempt to account for the relationship between level of education and participation in politics suggests an observation about general political socialization theory. Although certain basic aspects of the political self are established prior to adulthood, political learning continues beyond childhood and adolescence. The citizen's style of actual political participation is not firmly established by pre-adult socialization. It is during the adult years that opportunities become available for engagement in political activities. In this section we have reviewed how it is that tendencies toward active political involvement are linked to the resources and experiences most available to the better educated in society. Particular political socialization experiences, therefore, are distributed in society according to social status. This is a point we will pursue in greater detail in Chapter X.

THE SCHOOLS AND POLITICAL SOCIALIZATION

In most societies the school stands with the family and peer groups as one of the most significant agents of political learning. Under some conditions its influence is likely to be even greater than these other two socialization agents. Like the family, the school influences the child and adolescent during the crucial formative years. The school provides the adolescent citizen with knowledge about the political world and his role in it. It equips the child with more concrete perceptions of political institutions and relationships. The school also transmits the consensual values and attitudes of the society. Except in the case of special subgroup schools and youth organizations affiliated with political parties, the school has little direct effect on the development of partisan values or subgroup loyalties.

In contrast to the family and peer groups, schools are susceptible to centralized and uniform control. One of the key attributes of the family and peer groups as sources of political orientations, as we have said, is their tendency to be decentralized, nondeliberate, and haphazard. Schools, of course, operate differently. It is possible for a given regime to design, and in some instances to implement, a fairly uniform program of political education and indoctrination for the vast majority of the children and adolescents of an entire society. Common political values and information can be disseminated in a fairly uniform way to a large proportion of a nation's young people. Political socialization in the schools is often more deliberate than that of the family and peer groups. Most political regimes and educational administrators accept citizenship training and political indoctrination as an important part of education.

Although political education programs are more uniform, manipulable, and deliberate than the family and peer group teaching, they generally fall short of total control and uniform effect. Uniformity of program and intention seldom means uniformity of application. Even the most centralized school system has trouble manipulating all the politically relevant messages communicated in all of its classrooms. Even when there is uniformity of intention, different teachers and different classrooms are not equally effective. As we pointed out before, students differ in their receptiveness to political messages communicated in the classroom.

Despite the many factors working against uniform political socialization in the schools, schools remain one of the more controllable sources of political learning. A society seeking to bring about large-scale and rapid changes in political values will find the educational system among the most effective means for implementing uniform alterations. The leaders of totalitarian nations and of the new nations generally have accepted this and have expended resources in the development of schools and political education programs in them.

The potential influence of the school as a transmitter of political values was eloquently captured at the turn of the century by a school superintendent of an Eastern seaboard city, commenting on the task of socializing the large immigrant populations into the American way of life. His thoughts are an appropriate conclusion to this chapter.

> The public school is the greatest and most effective of all Americanization agencies. This is the one place where all children in a community or district, regardless of nationality, religion, politics, or social status, meet and work together in a cooperative and harmonious spirit. . . . The children work and play together, they catch the school spirit, they live the democratic life, American heroes become their own, American history wins their loyalty, the Stars and Stripes, always before their eyes in the school room, receives their daily salute.[59]

[59] Quoted in Robert Dahl, *Who Governs?* (New Haven: Yale University Press, 1961), pp. 316–317.

CHAPTER X

Social Groupings, Secondary Groups, Political Experiences, and Mass Media

WE HAVE DISCUSSED at some length the family, peer groups, and schools as transmitters and creators of political orientations. Although these agencies are generally the most important sources, other agents also influence political learning: (1) social groupings, such as class and race; (2) secondary groups, such as political organizations and occupational associations; (3) experiences with the political world; and (4) communication media. In this chapter we discuss briefly the part each of these plays in forming political orientations.

SOCIAL GROUPINGS AND POLITICAL ORIENTATIONS

The expression "social grouping" refers to the broad categories in the population. Societies are composed of a number of socially significant categories: social class, income level, occupation, race, religious affiliation, and national, regional, and tribal origin. Persons belong to these groupings because they have certain physical attributes, or hold specified beliefs, or belong to a particular social or occupational stratum.

In nearly all societies personal or family wealth is an important factor in assigning people to social groupings. In some nations (*e.g.,* Canada, Lebanon, Germany, and Holland), re-

ligious beliefs are important categories that order the population. National, regional, and tribal background categorize
people in the United States, the Soviet Union, Spain, Nigeria,
and Uganda. Race and caste are important social groupings in
the Republic of South Africa and India, respectively.

Social groupings are not the same as secondary groups.[1]
They lack the formal structures and processes which characterize secondary groups. A social grouping such as the working class in Britain, Negroes in the United States, and the
Christian population of Lebanon can, and should, be distinguished from a Labour Party club in England, the Congress on Racial Equality in the United States, and the
Lebanese Church as a religious organization. These organizations may draw their members from the respective social
groupings and presume to act as spokesmen for them, but they
are different phenomena. This distinction is important for
understanding the respective roles of social groupings and
secondary groups in the development of political orientations.
By and large this distinction has not been formulated adequately in the analysis of how social structures influence
political life.[2]

Social groupings have a tremendous influence on political
orientations. Study after study of party preferences, policy
choices, or level of political participation have shown that
persons in different classes, occupations, and income categories,
religions, geographic regions, and so on hold quite different
political views.[3] Social class variations are politically significant in Britain, Australia, Scandinavia, and most of Western

[1] The notion of group and its distinction from other collectivities of
people is discussed in Cecil A. Gibb, "Leadership," in Gardner Lindzey
(ed.), *Handbook of Social Psychology*, II (Reading, Mass.: Addison-Wesley,
1954), pp. 877–917.

[2] Much of the literature analyzing the effect of group life on political
life has thrown what we are calling "social groupings" and "secondary
groups" together under the label "group." This literature has been insen-
sitive to the particular way in which social groupings influence political
life.

[3] For summaries of this literature, see Lester W. Milbrath, *Political
Participation: How and Why Do People Get Involved in Politics?* (Chi-
cago: Rand McNally, 1965), Chapter 5; and S. M. Lipset, *Political Man*
(New York: Doubleday, 1960), Chapters 6–8.

Europe. Regional and ethnic factors are important in Canada, the United States, and Southern Europe. In the new nations of Africa, persistent tribal loyalties are often the source of political commitments.

The political relevance of these groupings is apparent early in life. The Hess and Torney analysis of social class differences among American elementary school children found little difference between children of different classes in regard to basic attachments to the nation and in general acceptance of law and authority. However, they did find that

> . . . lower status children more frequently accept authority figures as right and rely on their trustworthiness and benign intent. There is, therefore, more acquiescence to the formal structure and less tendency to question the motivations behind the behavior of government and governmental officials.[4]

Higher status children have higher levels of interest and a greater sense of efficacy in the political world. Social status background is related to party preferences beginning by about grade five, and becomes increasingly pronounced in successively higher grades.

The existence of these relationships is so well documented that there is no need to discuss them in detail here. The central issue for us is how they fit in with political socialization processes. How do these social and economic attachments take on political relevance? What causes these relationships to persist over time?

We know that a child gets his earliest and deepest political convictions from his family. Now we can go further and add that the social groupings to which his family belongs have a major influence on the political atmosphere in his home. A lower class family is less apt to engage in explicit political teaching than a middle or upper class family. A middle or upper class family, through example and direct indoctrination, is more likely to teach its children to be active in politics and to expect results from that activity than is a lower class

---

[4] Robert D. Hess and Judith V. Torney, *The Development of Political Attitudes in Children* (Chicago: Aldine Publishing Co., 1967), pp. 126–172.

family. In most societies lower class families pass on attitudes about politics and political parties that are different from those learned in middle and upper class families. In much of Latin America and rural Europe the Catholic Church teaches the peasant political acquiescence and conservatism. Student youth groups and urban labor unions in the same nations urge political change and activism. Whether the youth grows to political maturity in a traditional Catholic peasant village, a politically active university, in a proletarian setting makes a difference in how he fits into the political world.

The individual's position in social groupings determines, in large measure, what types of political learning experiences he will have. The tendency for members of common groupings to live, work, and socialize with each other restricts exposure to diverse socialization experiences. Because people in a particular social category, for the most part, make friends with "their own kind" of people, the political views they hear outside the family are usually very much like the ones they hear at home. These groupings, with their special slant on political matters, persist because parents pass on their sense of membership to their children. This sense of belonging in a particular social category, as we pointed out in Chapter VII, is something that parents manage to communicate to their children while the children are still very young.

Social groupings take on meaning for political life in another way as well. They serve as reference points or conceptual filters for the individual's understanding of the world of politics.[5] The individual forms attachments and identifications with social categories, and these identifications affect the way in which he perceives the world. Racial identification, social class identity, and other attachments in this sense become a part of the political self. They are basic components of self-interpretations and self-identifications. The Jew, for example, may come to identify with Jews or Jewishness and may see

[5] In recent social science literature this notion comes closest to the concept of a reference group, or what V. O. Key broadens into the concept of a reference symbol. See V. O. Key, Jr., *Public Opinion and American Democracy* (New York: Knopf, 1961), pp. 63–65; and Herbert H. Hyman, "Reflections on Reference Groups," *Public Opinion Quarterly*, XXIV (1960), pp. 383–396.

politics, including himself as a political subject or actor, from a Jewish reference point. He makes political evaluations and choices on the basis of a Jewish perspective, or Jewish interest.

The pattern of orientations that forms the political culture is determined to a great degree by the rigidity and consistency with which groupings divide a population.[6] In some societies members of different groupings differ markedly in political attachments and values. In Canada religious-ethnic ties sharply differentiate the political outlooks, including basic political attachments, of the French-Canadians from other Canadians. The French-Canadians, because they tend to share political values and loyalties that are different from those of the larger society, constitute a particular political subculture. Societies that have a number of distinctive and enduring political subcultures are said to have fragmented political cultures.[7]

In other societies variation in political outlooks by social groups is not great; a broad consensus exists on fundamental political values and objectives. The members of one social class or ethnic group share basic political attachments and values with those of other classes and groupings. When there is substantial agreement crossing over regional, rural-urban, occupational, and social class lines,[8] we say that society is a "consensual" society, or that it has a unified political culture.

The extent to which a society is consensual greatly affects political functioning and stability.

Stability is difficult to maintain in the midst of a severely fragmented political culture. Stable democracies seem most likely to develop in nonfragmented cultures in which there is broad consensus on political fundamentals.[9] This is not the place to discuss these issues in detail. We suggest in passing, however, that the pattern of social groupings is an important component of a political society, and that such patterns are created and perpetuated through political socialization.[10]

[6] See Gabriel Almond and Sidney Verba, *The Civic Culture* (Princeton: Princeton University Press, 1963), Chapters 14–15.

[7] *Ibid.*, pp. 27–29.

[8] V. O. Key, Jr., *op. cit.*, pp. 99–206.

[9] See Almond and Verba, *loc. cit.*, and Lipset, *op. cit.*, Chapter 3.

[10] Almond and Verba, *op. cit.*, Chapter 12.

SECONDARY GROUPS

Secondary groups act as agents of political learning in much the same way as peer groups, schools, and the family. Often they specifically instruct their members concerning political attitudes and behavior, they punish members to enforce political standards, mobilize individuals to participate in politics, and train persons for political life. Most societies contain a variety of secondary groups which regulate the activities and values of their members. Though the number and significance of such groups is in large part a function of the complexity and level of economic development of a society (the more highly developed and complex the society, the greater the number of secondary groups and the more important they are in social and political functions); [11] even the most primitive societies have brotherhoods, councils, and less formalized groups which play important roles in transmitting the lore and enforcing the rules of their cultures.

Although many different groups act as agencies for political learning, we can specify three types. These types of secondary groups differ in how deliberate, thorough, and successful they are in socializing, and they vary in the ways in which they are tied into the political world.

First, there are groups instituted specifically for political purposes, sometimes especially for political teaching and indoctrination. Political parties and youth groups are the most common and important of such groups. They are established to propagate political values, mobilize political action, and recruit political leaders. Specifically political groups rarely involve more than a small minority of citizens in their organizational life. Nevertheless, they are important because they touch the small number of persons who are concerned, active, and influential in political affairs and who in turn disseminate political information and values to other persons.

A second type consists of groups which are set up for non-political purposes, but which carry on political education and mobilization along with their other activities. Religious

[11] See David B. Truman, *The Governmental Process* (New York: Knopf, 1951), Chapter 3.

groups, occupational associations, and fraternal organizations (all established primarily for nonpolitical purposes) often in clude specific programs of political indoctrination among their group activities. Labor unions have political action and education departments as well as collective bargaining and member welfare divisions. Churches take stands and issue pronouncements on social and political affairs. Professional associations such as the American Medical Association devote time and resources to promoting political practices which serve their interests. Occupational associations are among the most universal and influential secondary groups with relevance for political outlooks in modern and modernizing societies. They involve large segments of the population of industrialized societies and are heeded by members because they touch on members' economic and professional interests. Because professional associations are related to occupational strata, they tend to promote occupational and class related political values, and, thus, to intensify social and economic cleavages.

A third category includes groups which perform political socialization as a less formal and programmed activity. Many secondary groups transmit political messages in informal ways and provide settings in which other forms of political learning take place. Little League baseball clubs do not have political indoctrination programs, but they do inculcate values which have political relevance. A country club or cricket club, though not including political education among its activities, does provide primary relationships in which political attitudes and values are formulated and transmitted.

Secondary groups affect political orientations in several ways. Some groups engage in direct political education and indoctrination efforts. They articulate norms and information about politics to members and often to nonmembers. In other cases participation in these groups is a source of indirect political learning, especially for the apprenticeship form discussed in Chapter V. Secondary groups provide a framework in which primary relationships develop, and those primary relationships, in turn, influence political outlooks. Secondary groups serve as reference points in much the same way that social groupings do. The first type of secondary group influence is fairly self-evident and does not require elaboration here. The others, however, merit brief discussion.

One important contribution that secondary groups make to political learning is to provide experiences and training in group relationships which can be transferred to the world of politics. Participation itself, regardless of the political content and purposes of the group, affects perceptions, skills, and relationships in the world of politics. Numerous studies have documented the notion that participation in secondary groups is associated positively with higher levels of political interest, involvement, participation, and with greater sense of political efficacy.[12] Participation generates skills, information, and predispositions that are useful for relationships in the political world. Almond and Verba summarize findings from their five-nation study bearing on this notion as follows:

> [Citizens] who are members of a nonpolitical organization are more likely to feel subjectively competent than are those who belong to no organization. This, then, appears to confirm the fact that latent political functions are performed by voluntary associations, whether those organizations are political or not. Those who are members of some organizations, even if they report that it has no political role, have more political competence than those who have no such membership.[13]

Political theorists have long commented on the relevance of voluntary group participation for the operation of liberal democratic societies.[14] The existence of such groups has been accepted by some as a requisite for stable pluralistic democracy. Although secondary groups may, at times, be sources

---

[12] For inventories of this literature, see Milbrath, *op. cit.*, pp. 130–133 and Robert E. Lane, *Political Life: Why People Get Involved in Politics* (New York: The Free Press, 1959), pp. 187–203; see also Sidney Verba, "Organizational Membership and Democratic Consensus," *Journal of Politics*, XXVII (1965), pp. 467–497.

[13] Almond and Verba, *op. cit.*, p. 309.

[14] See Alexis de Tocqueville, *Democracy in America*, II (New York: Vintage Books, 1945), especially pp. 114–118; William Kornhauser, *The Politics of Mass Society* (New York: The Free Press, 1959); S. M. Lipset, Martin Trow, and James Coleman, *Union Democracy: What Makes Democracy Work in Labor Organizations and Other Organizations?* (New York: The Free Press, 1956).

of conflicting influence and action, they help equip individuals with the political attitudes appropriate for democratic politics.[15]

Secondary groups also act as political reference groups. In this sense their influence on ideas and values is similar to that of social groupings. Individuals form identifications with a particular group such as a labor union, a farmers' organization, or a religious association, and use that group as a political reference point. They become sensitive to the group's political norms and make political evaluations according to what is best for the group and what it stands for. The same organization can be a positive reference group for some, a negative reference group for others. For the industrial worker, the union is a positive reference group; for the businessman it is a negative reference group. And so the industrial worker votes for the union's values and interests, and the businessman is likely to be against anything the union is for.[16] The Communist Party has long been a negative reference group for many Americans. In recent years the John Birch Society and the Ku Klux Klan also have become negative reference groups whose support many candidates for public office disavow.

Many primary relationships are formed within the context of secondary groups. Individuals brought together in the activities of a secondary group often form primary ties with one another. Adolescent and youth groups, such as scout troops and students or religious movements, provide youth with contacts that grow into primary groups. Adult primary associations likewise develop within work and social organizations. Secondary groups, thus, structure the individual activity and social relationships which can have such a bearing on political views.

In the chapter on peer groups we commented more extensively on this relationship between primary and secondary groups, pointing out that primary groups relate individual members to their various secondary groups. Primary associates often pull members into the group, tell them how things are

---

[15] See Tocqueville, *loc. cit.*; and Kornhauser, *loc. cit.*
[16] For a discussion of reference groups see Hyman, *loc. cit.*

done, and punish deviant behavior.[17] Here we stress the opposite causal chain of influence. Secondary groups provide frameworks and contacts within which primary relationships develop. The primary groups serve to communicate and develop political orientations, often without regard to the political objectives of the larger group. A loyal Democrat, for instance, may join a religious group for the appropriate religious reasons and become active in its group life. He may establish close personal friendships among several members of the group. Because of his strong political interests and partisan ties he may talk politics with these coreligionists. He influences the political outlook of these friends because they are friends.

We have outlined various methods through which secondary groups influence the content and structure of the political self. Obviously, the several modes are not mutually exclusive. They often act simultaneously and reinforce each other. The propositions outlined in Chapter VIII to describe the differential influence of primary groups on political outlooks are generally applicable to secondary groups as well.[18] The more important the group is for the individual, and the more closely he is related to it, the more likely the group is to influence his political outlook. The more active the group is in communicating political views, and the more the individual regards the group as politically relevant, the more it shapes political orientations.[19]

Secondary groups are influential particularly during youth and adulthood, as the influence of family and school wanes. For that reason they are most influential for the types of learning that occur after childhood. Secondary groups are important in perpetuating and reinforcing political values re-

[17] See Bernard R. Berelson, Paul F. Lazarsfeld, and William N. McPhee, *Voting* (Chicago: University of Chicago Press, 1954), p. 94.

[18] For a more detailed discussion and propositional inventory on group impact on political attitudes and behavior, see Richard E. Dawson, *The Local Union and Political Behavior: Some Aspects of Group Influence on Individual Attitudes and Behavior*, unpublished doctoral dissertation, Northwestern University, 1963, especially Chapter 2.

[19] See Angus Campbell, Philip E. Converse, Warren E. Miller, and Donald E. Stokes, *The American Voter* (New York: Wiley, 1960), Chapter 12.

lated to the social and economic groupings discussed above. In this sense they help maintain the distribution of political orientations linked to the social and demographic structure of societies.[20]

POLITICAL EVENTS AND POLITICAL EXPERIENCES

Up to now we have emphasized nonpolitical institutions and experiences in the development of the political self. We have concentrated on the family, primary groups, and schools — all agencies whose major functions are socialization, education, and personal relationships. Only in rare instances are these directly a part of formal political structures. This emphasis is justifiable since a major portion of political learning takes place in these general socialization agencies. They are important particularly for the early stages of political maturation.

We should not, however, overlook the direct impact of the political world on political perceptions and values. Political learning, quite obviously, does not occur in isolation from the world of politics. During his early years the maturing citizen learns *about* a political world with which he has little direct contact and few direct relationships. The child is taught by family and schools what voting is, but only as an adult does he actually vote. Many of the lessons about politics are learned by the child in anticipation of his rights and responsibilities as an adult. On the whole, political experiences come after basic political learning is accomplished. We do not mean to imply that the child has no direct experience with the political world. He is familiar with some political symbols and personalities and hears about some political events. Nevertheless, such experiences are not the major aspect of early political learning. By late adolescence and after, political experiences themselves enter the stage to help shape the political self. The individual begins to learn directly from the political world,

[20] This point, obviously, must be qualified. Some secondary groups, such as the Boy Scouts and numerous civic associations, concentrate on teaching consensus values rather than partisan or group-oriented values. Nonetheless the overall effect of secondary groups is to support group interests and group oriented orientations.

instead of only about it. Political leaders attempt to influence his attitudes by speeches, announcements, and propaganda campaigns. Political events such as revolutions, assassinations, or elections, often directly affect political values and beliefs. Voting, attending political meetings, dealing with governmental officials, provide important lessons for the individual citizen.

To some extent adult experiences in the political world are a sort of testing of reality. In childhood and youth the citizen is taught many things about his political world. This learning later is tested by his actual experiences. As a child he may be taught that political leaders are wise and benevolent; that he should trust, respect, and obey them. In later experiences he finds they make unwise decisions and do not treat citizens fairly. The child is taught in school that the policeman is a friendly, fair, and trustworthy helper. Later experiences at the hands of the law may teach him that the police are brutal and dishonest. Of course, political experiences are not always disenchanting. A young man may be taught by his father that governmental bureaucrats won't listen to him, and that it is useless to expect any services from them. The youth, with more education and social status than his father, may learn later how to approach public officials and find them responsive to his petitions. But given the nature of official political education in most nations, with its tendency to simplify and glorify the political images presented, actual political experiences are more likely to develop cynicism than vice versa.

Studies of American school children find that children tend to have positive, benevolent attitudes toward political authority figures.[21] They are not cynical about government. Political cynicism, however, is widespread among American adults.[22] Another seeming anomaly is that lower class children more frequently accept authority figures as right and depend on their trustworthiness.[23] But among the adult population

[21] See Fred I. Greenstein, *Children and Politics* (New Haven: Yale University Press, 1965), pp. 31–42.

[22] Robert E. Aggar, Marshall Goldstein, and Stanley Pearl, "Political Cynicism: Meaning and Measurements," *Journal of Politics*, XXIII (1961), pp. 477–506.

[23] Robert D. Hess and Judith Torney, *loc. cit.*

it is the citizens of higher status who demonstrate more trust and have the more positive attitudes toward governmental effectiveness and toward their own efficacy in the political world. There appears, then, to be a reversal in class tendencies between childhood and adulthood, with lower status citizens becoming more cynical and less positive about the political world. We suggest that this reversal results in part from the different experiences upper and lower status persons have in the political and social world. The experiences of lower status citizens lead them to become more cynical about politics and less sure about their ability to influence the political world. The political experiences of higher status persons, on the other hand, lead them to become more positive and to develop a greater sense of political efficacy because they have been more successful.

Political experiences and political events are obviously most important for those who have an interest in politics. Political events are less likely to influence people who are isolated from the political mainstream and those who have only minimal perceptions of the political world. There are data suggesting that the political activists tend to have political values somewhat different from the rest of the population.[24] Key proposes the existence of a political activist subculture made up of the minority of citizens who are particularly attentive to and active in politics.[25] He suggests that this minority has more confidence in democratic procedures than the rest of society. If this is true, it probably follows that experiences in the political world, as well as experiences with socialization agents, play an especially important part in forming views of the political activists.

Since we discussed in Chapter IV ways in which political experiences shape the political self, a detailed discussion is not needed here. To summarize: political events and experiences in the political world are particularly important for the political learning that takes place during the adult years. Political socialization of this type is most significant for the

---

[24] See especially Robert McClosky, "Consensus and Ideology in American Politics," *American Political Science Review*, LVIII (1964), pp. 361–382.
[25] V. O. Key, Jr., *op. cit.*, pp. 536–558.

readjustments the individual makes with the changing political world. His experiences serve to correct or complete the political learning that took place during the preadult years. Learning from political experiences and events is most important for the politically attentive and active.

COMMUNICATION MEDIA

Newspapers, radio, television, magazines, and other communication media transmit many types of messages which affect political orientations. Both day-to-day information about political events and evaluations of these events are transmitted from government to citizen, from group to group, from group to individual, from elite to nonelite, through the communication media. As a result of technological advancements in communication media and the weakening of traditional social structures like the extended family and the local community, the mass media are becoming increasingly important as shapers of political orientations.

The modern nation-state with its common political focus, centralized administration, and widespread participation could not have developed without the advancements in the technology of mass communication.[26] The modern integrated polity cannot exist without widespread, rapid, and generally uniform communication. The rapidity and scope of modern communication was demonstrated vividly at the time of the assassination of President Kennedy in November, 1963. Within a few hours almost all Americans knew about the president's death.[27] The news was spread with similar rapidity to nearly all corners of the world. It is accurate to say that most of the world responded simultaneously to a common event.

Even as the mass media are a crucial ingredient for the modern state, they are also an important mechanism through which traditional societies move toward modernity and political integration. Because the mass media can disseminate a con-

[26] See Reinhard Bendix, *Max Weber: An Intellectual Portrait* (New York: Doubleday, 1960), Chapters 12–13.

[27] See Paul B. Sheatsley and Jacob J. Feldman, "The Assassination of President Kennedy: A Preliminary Report on Public Reactions and Behavior," *Public Opinion Quarterly*, XXVIII (1964), pp. 192–193.

sistent and standardized political message s'
vast numbers of people, they can play a ke
transformation of society. Hyman points o.
tional societies, the media, as instruments of socia.

> efficient and their sweep is vast enough to cover the huge po.
> ulations requiring modernization. Their standardization . . . is
> suited to producing widespread national uniformities in pat-
> terns of behavior; and their spirit is modern, no matter what
> else is wrong with it. By contrast, while the conventional agen-
> cies of socialization in society — parents, teachers, peers, neigh-
> bors, and the like — can be more flexible in suiting the lesson
> to the capacities and needs of the particular learner and more
> potent an influence, the outcomes cannot be as uniform, and
> their efforts are often directed against modernization.[28]

Hyman is correct in stressing the potential utility of mass
media for the tasks of modernization and integration, but their
potential in this capacity is easily overrated. The same societies
that Hyman believes require standardized socialization are
those which lack the technical skills and facilities to use the
mass media effectively. The nations most in need of such
modernizing communication are those least likely to have such
resources. Their populations often are illiterate, possess few
radios and television sets, and are inattentive to the political
content of media communications.

The mass media are more prevalent and effective as instruments of communication and socialization in more modern
societies.[29] This point is testified to by data presented in Table
X.1. The mass media, particularly television and movies, are
the most frequently mentioned sources of information about
foreign people for children in the modern nations e.g., the
United States, Canada, Germany, and Japan. In the less well
developed societies — Bantu (Republic of South Africa), Brazil,
Israel, Lebanon, and Turkey — television is not mentioned at

[28] Herbert H. Hyman, "Mass Communication and Political Socialization: The Role of Patterns of Communications," in Lucien Pye (ed.),
Communications and Political Development (Princeton: Princeton University Press, 1963), p. 143.

[29] See Richard R. Fagen, *Politics and Communication* (Boston: Little,
Brown, 1966), pp. 53–69.

TABLE X.1 *Comparisons of Popularly Used Sources of Information (About Foreign People)*

Nationality of Children

	American	Bantu	Brazilian	English-Canadian	French	French-Canadian	German	Israeli	Japanese	Lebanese	Turkish
6-year-olds	TV movies (parents)	parents	parents (contact)	TV,[b] contact	parents	TV[b]	parents, TV-movies (contact)	parents, friends	parents, TV-movies	contact, parents	parents, friends
10- and 14-year-olds	TV-movies, books, courses, texts, magazines	parents, (10 yrs. only), contact,[c] teachers	movies, magazines, contact	TV, courses, texts, books	parents (10 yrs. only), texts, books, magazines, (14 yrs. only)	TV, texts, books, magazines (14 yrs. only)	TV-movies, books, magazines, courses, contact, radio	books, friends, courses, movies, magazines	TV-movies, courses, texts, teachers, magazines	books, magazines, radio, movies, texts, friends, contact	books, texts, courses, movies, magazines

a Listed in approximate order of frequency. Those in parentheses are not as frequently mentioned as the others.

b Since children in Montreal are not allowed to attend movie theatres until they are 16 years of age, it was presumed that television was the major source coded in the TV-movies category.

c Refers to direct contact or exposure to foreign people.

Source: *Children's Views of Foreign Peoples, A Cross-National Study*, by Wallace E. Lambert and Otto Klineberg. Copyright © 1967 by Meredith Publishing Company. Reprinted by permission of Appleton-Century-Crofts.

all. Parents and friends are the most frequently mentioned information sources. France is the only important exception to this pattern. France is a highly developed nation in an economic sense, but it follows the patterns of the less developed nations in regard to information sources. Even as these data suggest differences in communication patterns between modern and nonmodern societies, they attest to an important role for the mass media, especially television, in more highly developed nations.

In evaluating mass media as a political socialization agency *important* four observations are relevant. First, more often than not the media act as transmitters of political cues which are originated by other agencies. Second, the information carried by mass media goes through a two-step flow. Third, the media tend to reinforce existing political orientations rather than create new ones. Fourth, the messages of the mass media are received and interpreted in a social setting, and in the context of socially conditioned predispositions.

Many of the politically relevant messages transmitted through radio, television, newspapers, and other communication media have their origins outside the media. Government officials and political leaders make statements; secondary groups transmit political information to their members; events in the political world are picked up and communicated to large populations. The media serve mainly as the instrument through which these socialization agencies communicate their messages. The directors of mass media may, in fact, have only a limited say in what sort of political data they transmit to the population.

A number of communication studies have found that mass communication media do not tend to influence the masses of the population directly.[30] Messages coming through the media first reach a small number of "opinion leaders" who are particularly attentive to the media. By word of mouth, opinion leaders such as teachers, ministers, community activists, etc., then pass on the messages to those over whom they are in-

[30] For summaries of this work see Elihu Katz, "The Two-Step Flow of Communication: An Up-to-Date Report on an Hypothesis," *Public Opinion Quarterly*, XXI (1957), pp. 61–78; and Elihu Katz and Paul F. Lazarsfeld, *Personal Influence* (New York: The Free Press, 1955).

fluential. Mass media messages, thus, tend to flow in two steps. The opinion leader is the crucial person; he usually influences a small group of close friends. Katz describes the relationship as follows:

> Opinion leaders and the people whom they influence are very much alike and typically belong to the same primary groups of family, friends and co-workers. While the opinion leader may be more interested in the particular sphere in which he is influential, it is highly unlikely that the persons influenced will be very far behind the leader in their level of interest.[31]

We discussed the notion of the two-step flow of communication in the chapter on peer groups. This mechanism places additional emphasis upon the family and peer groups as influential agents of political learning. Only a minority of persons follow the media closely, especially the political communications there. Those who do are important in communicating the messages to those who don't. In the process, of course, the message gets reinterpreted and transformed by the opinion leaders.

On the whole, the mass media serve to reinforce existing orientations rather than to alter old ones or create new ones. As one student of communication's influence points out: "A number of studies, some performed in the laboratory and some in the social world, indicate that persuasive mass communication functions far more frequently as an agent of reinforcement than as an agent of change." [32] In his study of public opinion, Key sets this observation in a larger social context. He points out that: ". . . it is safe to conclude that the major influence of the media upon political attitudes is by and large a reinforcement of the status quo." [33]

This reinforcement of existing orientations results in part from the nature of communication messages. Major messages are designed for the most part to support existing arrangements and to convey interpretations considered appropriate by

[31] Katz, "The Two-Step Flow," p. 77.

[32] Joseph T. Klapper, *The Effects of Mass Communication* (New York: The Free Press, 1960), p. 15.

[33] Key, *op. cit.*, p. 396.

social power holders. This reinforcement function results also from tendencies on the part of the receiver. People are more apt to be attentive to the media when they agree with what they are being told. During a political campaign people pay attention to the speeches of the candidates they already support. A study of the effect of an educational campaign on the United Nations, for example, found that those who noticed the campaign were those who were most favorably disposed toward the United Nations before the campaign.[34] Those not favorable to the United Nations, the ones who the campaign set out to influence, tended not to notice or be affected by the educational effort. The communication media, consequently, are *not* the most effective means of converting persons to new ideas. Messages may be sent out, but there is no way of ensuring that they will reach those to whom they are directed. Katz and Lazarsfeld offer the following conclusion about the persuasive influence of the media: "Perhaps the most important generalization in this area — at least as far as understanding the process of effective persuasion is concerned — is that those groups which are most hopefully regarded as the target of a communication are often least likely to be in the audience." [35]

As the two-step flow of communication hypothesis suggests, messages from the mass media are seldom received and interpreted by isolated individuals. The reaction to mass media communications are influenced by the social location of the individual receiving them. Both the individual's preconceptions and his immediate social setting influence the impact that mass media will have on him.[36] First, the social setting helps determine which media and communications the individual will be exposed to. Second, the social setting affects the way in which the individual interprets and reacts to particular messages. "It is obvious that mass communication is a social process — a social person interacts with others, participates in

34 S. A. Star and H. M. Hughes, "Report on an Educational Campaign: The Cincinnati Plan for the United Nations," *American Journal of Sociology*, LV (1950), pp. 389–440.

35 Katz and Lazarsfeld, *op. cit.*, pp. 21–22.

36 See Eliot Friedson, "The Relation of the Social Situation of Contact to the Media in Mass Communication," *Public Opinion Quarterly*, XVII (1953), pp. 230–238.

cooperative social activities." [37] This observation again stresses the importance of primary associations and personal influences in the development of political outlooks.

These four qualifications constitute a brief outline of factors relevant to the socialization influence of mass communication media. By and large they suggest that the media affect the development of attitudes and opinions primarily in conjunction with other agents of socialization, especially small, personal groups. The communication media are important in carrying numerous political messages, the most important of which are news about everyday political events. In addition, the media convey, both directly and indirectly, the major consensus values of the society. Media act to reinforce the lessons passed on, probably more effectively, by the family, schools, peers, and other agents of political learning.

[37] *Ibid.*, p. 230.

An Overview of the Process

IN THE PREVIOUS SECTIONS — one on the processes and the other on the agencies of political socialization — we made little attempt to tie together systematically the various findings and hypotheses considered. We recognize that data limitations make it premature to suggest a theory of political maturation or of political socialization. From the standpoint of comprehensive and comparative theory the most critical limitations have to do with the cultural and temporal biases of data currently available. Few political socialization studies allow for the comparison of one culture with another, with similar data on common issues. A large proportion of the data on political learning, as the reader cannot help but notice, has been taken from studies of American society. Even fewer studies have examined political socialization processes as they change over time. Because we are bounded by temporal constraints, we can offer only tentative hypotheses and conclusions. We have qualified our discussion with these limitations in view.

We have for the most part ignored questions about the way in which political socialization processes affect the operation of the polity. We suspect, of course, that the influence of political socialization includes more than the formation of the citizen's political views. Every dimension of the polity — public order, justice, legitimacy, policy, stability, leadership — is affected by the processes of political socialization and the structures through which this process occurs. However, just as it is premature to suggest a theory of political socialization, it is not yet possible to attempt a comprehensive statement on the consequences for political society of different socialization patterns.

Although we recognize these limitations, we do not want to be unduly narrow or cautious in our concluding formulations. There is value in pulling together the various findings in an effort to identify and summarize general patterns and to point out implications for the polity. In this chapter we will suggest some dimensions of a tentative, but comprehensive, overview, intended to collect political socialization findings and put them into a logical order.

More specifically, the summary links three aspects of political learning: (1) types of political orientations making up the political self, (2) chronological patterns of political maturation, (3) the varying effect of major agencies of political socialization. We include, then, attention to the product, the processes, and the agents of political socialization. In addition, we make some abbreviated references to the implications of political socialization for the total political society.

Before presenting these concluding formulations, it is best to offer a brief statement as to what we are and are not about. The aim is a summary, hypothetical description of political socialization in general. In Max Weber's words we are engaged in "ideal type" analysis. As such, we suggest something other than an empirically accurate description of political socialization for a specific set of individuals or for a given society. The cultural basis of most of the data drawn upon in this discussion, as well as the background (and socialization) of the authors, does mean, however, that the summary statement will be more reflective of American society than any other. Essentially, our summary is an abstraction constructed from observations of the empirical world, but not intended to replicate perfectly any one system of political socialization. Although neither a comprehensive theory nor an adequate empirical description, a summary statement of this type does point in a general way to the most important variables and relationships relevant to understanding political socialization.

In identifying central tendencies, we must overlook cultural variations. Not enough information is available to judge accurately how universal the components of this summary are. We also are avoiding normative questions. Although issues of "oughts" and "betters" flow from much of what we say, we do not discuss here whether what we identify as central tendencies are the most "appropriate" or "efficient" pattern of political socialization and whether such a pattern is beneficial or detrimental.

CENTRAL PATTERNS

1. *From Basic to Less Basic Orientations*. It is not necessary to review at length the framework presented in Chapter II and used in subsequent chapters. Children acquire early the basic interpretive orientations through which political happenings and perceptions are filtered. Only later in life does the citizen fully appreciate the institutional complexities of political life. It is even later that the citizen comes to understand and appreciate his role as a participant in the political life of his nation.

The most critical basic orientation is apparently an emotionally charged sense of belonging to a particular political community. We use such words as "patriotism" and "national loyalty" to capture the kind of relationships citizens develop at an early age with their political community. Similar types of orientations are acquired regarding other political institutions and symbols and various social groups. These also are learned at an early age. In substantial ways, these basic orientations influence what the individual comes to believe about politics in later life. These beliefs are referred to as "interpretive" orientations with good reason. It is through them that political events, personalities, and programs are interpreted, or come to "make sense." Without this foundation, the citizen's varying relationships with the political world would be uncomfortable. He would have no way of sorting the many political stimuli which reach him. He would find it difficult to make sense of the variety of political events and ideas which confront him. It is largely upon this basic interpretive framework that the average citizen's political self is built.

As the material we have presented makes clear, the family transmits most of the basic interpretative orientations. The family — supplemented by early peer groups and by school experiences — is at center stage during the initial years of political learning. During these formative years much of the child's political learning is indirect and unintentional. He picks up views regarding the political world from things said in the family. He transfers values derived from the family to other social settings.

The family continues to affect political outlooks throughout the life of the individual, but it does not retain its exclusive position for long. It soon comes to share influence with peer groups and, especially, with the school. The school is the first public agency of socialization the child encounters. In most societies schools bolster and extend the key political orientations, especially those centering on national loyalty and the society's consensus values.

From childhood on, the individual adds information and understanding to these basic orientations; he picks up more concrete information. These cognitive orientations help him find his way in the political world. He develops critical faculties and learns to evaluate the meaning of what he learns politically. By early adolescence, peer groups become more important in socialization, taking on a significance they retain through adult life. During this stage, political teaching is more deliberate. Schooling experiences attempt directly and systematically to ensure that the maturing child acquires political values and information appropriate for adult citizenship.

Finally, in later years, more political socialization takes place through secondary groups, mass media, and direct experiences with the political world. The family and the school have become less influential by late adolescence and young adulthood. Peer groups, however, retain substantial influence. As we have pointed out, the political self now begins to respond more directly to particular political programs and personalities. To borrow from the terminology of David Easton, it is primarily the citizen's relationship with government personalities and immediate issues, rather than the political community as a whole or the political institutions, which is affected by late adolescent and adult political socialization. For the most part, the citizen's response to particular political objects is affected by the basic interpretative orientations acquired early in life and the political information which fills out these orientations. One example is obvious: While quite young, an American child might learn from his family that to be a Democrat is "good," to be a Republican is "not good"; and that he is a Democrat and not a Republican. Subsequently, the child learns that to be a Democrat is to favor certain types of social legislation and group interests to the exclusion of others. As an adult, he votes a Democratic ticket. He formulates opinions on policy issues by following the lead of Democratic leaders. His adult political behavior is the logical extension of values, knowledge, and identifications formed during childhood and youth. This simple and linear example is repeated with many variations in regard to a host of other types of political orientations and behavior.

This general description of the incremental development of a political self, built on the values and identifications learned early in life, has characterized much of what we have suggested about political learning.

2. *The Differential Influence of Various Agencies.* As the individual matures politically, there is a waxing and waning pattern to the influence of various socialization agents. Roughly speaking, agencies of political learning fall into three categories. The first consists of agencies which have authority over the growing child. The parents and teacher are the most important examples. In the second category are agencies which stand in positions of equality with the learner. Age peers in school, friendship cliques in youth, and work associates in later life, as well as some relations in secondary groups, are examples of these types. In the third category are political experiences themselves. Having contact with political authorities, voting, paying taxes, obeying laws, receiving benefits, and so forth, are examples of such political socialization experiences. The political happenings that one learns about through the media are in this category also.

The earliest political socialization agencies are those which exert direct control over the child. At this early stage, the child is the recipient — mostly passive — of messages, cues, instructions, and directives. He imitates his elders in their political values and behavior. In his desire to be like those he looks up to, he takes on their characteristics. In the initial stages of developing a political self, the individual for the most part absorbs the political values of the older generation. The older generation, whether intentionally or not, transmits political orientations to the impressionable child. Continuity from one generation to the next is thus programmed into the political socialization process.

Later in life the individual operates on a more equal basis with political socialization agencies; by then he has formed many of the core orientations which shape his learning. Agents which stand on an equal footing with the learner are mostly responsible for adding specific content to the basic interpretative framework. It is from more nearly equal relationships that the citizen picks up much of the special knowledge and attitudes that make effective political life possible.

During adult years some of the most important political socialization experiences are likely to be those in which the citizen comes into direct contact with the political world. This is a period of testing reality. If predispositions carried to this point from early life turn out to be inadequate, basic alterations may occur. The political world often fails to operate as the young citizen had expected it to. Cynicism may replace unquestioning trust. Disillusionment may replace naive optimism. Conversely, the young adult may learn the value of political participation, though as a child he was taught its futility.

For the most part, the reality testing stage of political maturation will call for only marginal adjustments. Except where the political learning of childhood proves to be drastically inadequate, because the political situation has changed or the adult's social position has altered, the adult years add to the political self attitudes relevant for direct participation in political life.

During the citizen's adult years political socialization may be said to come full circle. The new adult, now a parent himself, passes on to his children the political values he has acquired. There may be some difference between what the parent learned as a child and what he transmits to his own child. However, the differences in most instances will be slight. Whereas parents often want their children to move beyond their status in an economic and social sense, few parents seem to wish for their children a political ideology different from their own.

This observation helps us to understand continuity in the political life of many societies. Older generations teach most intently those things they value most highly. Older generations are seldom indifferent to what the younger generation believes. For the parents and teachers to be indifferent would be to treat their own values as unimportant. Man links his self-esteem to confidence in his own values. He wants to protect the things he believes in and he wants to leave something of himself behind. That is why parents take such pains to teach their own values and attachments to their children. The twin drives of wanting to protect one's own values and wanting to procreate make all men teachers of the young.

The dynamics of value transmission are most in evidence when the values are important. Much of the material presented in our essay indicates that political values such as nationalism, patriotism, ethnic identification, and even partisan attachments are indeed very important. Since most individuals mature politically according to the patterns established when they are children, in many important respects each successive generation mirrors its predecessor. Political views, like religious beliefs, have considerable durability across generations.

Perpetuation of the status quo is not an inevitable outcome of the political socialization process; it is merely a highly probable one. Political socialization usually leads to continuity from one generation to the next because adults try to make sure that the young are taught the "right" political values. Churches, schools, homes, scouts, puberty rites, playgrounds, books, indeed every social institution and situation which bear some responsibility for socialization, assist in this task.

We have presented a developmental profile of the political self. There is a pattern of movement from a situation in which most teaching is done by those who have authority over the child, to a second stage, at which learning occurs under conditions of equal status, to a third stage, at which reality testing in the world of politics is the most important type of political learning. This cycle tends to be repeated in each generation. The more basic political loyalties are learned in childhood and then retaught when yesterday's child becomes today's parent.

This developmental cycle is the most significant point we offer in this essay. To further illustrate and clarify this plea, we will now devote our attention to a major political orientation, the attitude toward authority, and examine the cycle for this specific aspect of political learning.

Politics has to do with the organization and operation of power and authority in society. This, of course, is not all of politics, nor is politics the only aspect of life that involves the organization of power. Nevertheless, power and authority are central elements of the political world. A key aspect of political socialization is learning first to obey authority and subsequently discovering how to play a part in its direction and manipulation. For this reason attitudes toward authority serve as a good example of how the political self develops.

Early childhood development can be characterized as movement from a stage in which there is no recognition of rules and authority to a second stage in which rules are recognized as absolute — directed by some higher authority. This development is relevant for political socialization. Without obedience or adherence to authority, there is no social order. Unless a child learns to obey rules and regulations, he cannot take his place as a citizen in the adult world. Thus it is that adults teach children that obedience to authority is necessary and generally good. A child's first contact with government is characterized by this recognition of authority, of rules, of the necessity of obedience. Political objects are positive and emotionally charged. It is "good" to be good. Being good is being obedient. The law abiding basis of adult citizenship is laid early. Only later in the development of the political self do other views of authority take their place along with compliance.

As the child leaves the exclusive family circle and moves into peer groups and into the classroom, his experiences with authority undergo a subtle but significant change. Rules come to be seen as conventions, as something which are agreed upon though sometimes arbitrary. The child finds out that it is possible to ask questions about the rules. Rules cease to have the absolute character that they once had. Authorities "justify" their orders. We do not wish to exaggerate this point, however. Teachers continue to say, "do this because I say so." Power and authority remain mixed in the mind of the child. Nevertheless, the political socialization process is expanded to include other types of learning experiences, other perceptions of authority. We can see this trend accelerated, in particular, as we move from childhood into adolescence. Learning shifts from situations in which the learner is always submissive to situations in which he may be an equal. A new view of authority may come about first in peer groups, in which relationships are more spontaneous and rules less rigid and prevalent.

From a recognition of the conventional nature of rules comes another stage: the recognition that rules are changeable, that they can be influenced and manipulated. This recognition begins in adolescence, and is accelerated during early adulthood. We have cited the significance of extracurricular activities and participation in classroom decision making in earlier chapters. In addition, the political content of high school curricula tends to stress the participatory rights of individuals, in contrast to the passive duties of individuals stressed in lower grades. Authorities become somewhat redefined. Rather than distant, unapproachable law-givers, they become responsible and responsive leaders. Discussions of accountability replace instructions in obedience. As adolescence gives way to adulthood, this notion that authority is somewhat under the control or influence of the average citizen is even more prevalent. It is during the adult years that a person actually learns how to participate in politics, how to make his influence felt, how to voice demands, how to combine his claims with similar claims of others so as to maximize influence. Very often this learning takes place through doing.

The development of the citizen, from this perspective, can be viewed as a series of changes in attitudes toward power and authority. At the earliest stage, political learning stresses the "given" nature of authority. Later the stress is on the "conventional" nature, and still later the emphasis shifts to the "accountable" and "participatory" nature of authority. A basic and enduring respect for the political order is the foundation upon which orientations about the manipulability of specific rules are built.

The reader may be thinking of many cases that contradict the picture presented here. The example is biased heavily in the direction of participatory democracy. It may be a peculiarly American version. In other types of political systems the evolution of attitudes toward political authority will follow different patterns. The illustration is used merely to stress the developmental nature of political orientations, and to demonstrate how different agents play varying roles at different stages. The generic process illustrated is relevant, of course, to orientations other than views toward authority.

The example of how citizens come to view authority is instructive for another purpose, as well. The developmental profile permits us to analyze one of the major ways in which political socialization processes affect other political patterns in democratic societies.

An interesting question about any polity is why people obey political authority. The question is particularly critical in a democracy. The democratic philosophy informs the citizen that he is not obliged to conform to the law unless the law is generally to his liking. From Locke, from Rousseau, from Jefferson, indeed from the entire democratic tradition, we learn that democracies are built on the notion of "contingent obligation." A philosophy of contingent obligation means that the citizen can decide, "This is not for me, I'll emigrate (or secede)." Or, "I think I'll not pay taxes this year"; or "I'm tired of obeying traffic signals"; or "I refuse to be drafted." Needless to say, a system built upon the idea of contingent obligation might be a fragile one indeed.

We might ask then if democratic states practice what they preach. Does the citizen really believe in contingent obligation? Political socialization theory provides a partial answer and in so doing provides a clue to why some democracies operate as effectively as they often do.

We have seen that the young citizen first learns the lesson

of obedience as submission and only later learns that authority is conventional; not until adulthood does he really discover that he can participate in the making of binding decisions. It is critical here that the *first* lesson is that of unquestioned obedience. If we recall other material presented in the previous chapters, it is clear that another major lesson is learned at the same time as the lesson of obedience. This is the lesson of loyalty. Indeed, and this is the crux of the issue, the lessons of obedience and loyalty are indistinguishable. Children are taught to obey authority and to love their country at the same time and by the same models of behavior. They come to believe that it is "good" to "obey." The psychological link between obedience and loyalty in the mind of the citizen is significant for the way in which the political society operates.

First, of all the mechanisms which might induce obligation, political socialization is the cheapest and most efficient. In general people obey because they fear the consequence of disobedience, or because they consider it worth their while to obey, or because they consider compliance the appropriate behavior. The third reason, usually referred to as the sense of legitimacy, is the product of the type of political socialization processes discussed here. Fear and expedience, the alternative methods of inducing compliance, are expensive in comparison. Police states must spend a great deal on institutions which keep the populace in line. Expedience can be nearly as expensive. Under such conditions, authorities must continually make it worthwhile for the citizen to obey, and the "worth" in "worthwhile" comes dear. But compliance based on the feeling that obedience is "good" or "appropriate" is cheap. When authorities can depend on such a mechanism, they can direct resources and energies toward other goals.

Another implication is equally critical. This consequence of a political socialization process linking obedience to loyalty can also be viewed from the perspective of the citizen rather than the authorities. Democratic philosophy insists on the rights of minorities. Theoretically, one of the minority rights, by no means an unimportant one, is secession. A sizable minority in any democratic national system which becomes dissatisfied with the political order should be able to opt out.

Of course, secession as a tenet of democratic ideology conflicts with the demands of nationalism. Nationalism insists on protecting the integrity of the territorial boundaries. Neither encroachments from without nor mass emigration from within nor secession of any geographical entity is tolerable to the nation-state. In a very real sense, "compulsory citizenship" is not unknown in democratic nations.

How do citizens, especially members of potentially disgruntled minority groups, come to accept compulsory citizenship? Few American Negroes, for example, speak of leaving the national system. Findings presented earlier provide the answer to this question. Compulsory citizenship is made tolerable because the sense of loyalty to the nation-state is deeply imbedded. The basic inconsistency between democratic philosophy and nationalistic ideology is infrequently perceived by the citizen, and even less frequently acted upon. The multitude of political socialization agencies are largely responsible for creating and sustaining the sense of patriotism which conveniently connects obedience and loyalty.

As our summarizing framework indicates, the citizen does eventually learn that authority is not "given," but is accountable. But by the time he discovers this, his ties with the nation are firmly cemented. In the overwhelming majority of cases citizens do not revolt against the political order, even when the official ideology gives them this right.

In other words, the remarkable thing about democracies is that in assuming a policy of contingent obligation, they generate so few problems of disaffection and withdrawal. The reason for this is that most nations really do not permit the citizen's sense of obligation to be contingent. Political socialization mechanisms replace fear or purchase as a way of maintaining citizenship loyalty. The earliest models of citizenship — parents, teachers, youth leaders, ministers — are models of obedience. Our cultural heroes are not those who violate the norms but those who uphold them. Citizens become bound to the political community with such psychological tenacity that the option of noncompliance is seldom raised.

3. *The Informality of Political Socialization.* Much of what an individual learns about the political world he learns from

socialization agencies and social experiences which are only indirectly linked to the formal political system. The family and peer groups, in particular, are beyond the direct control and manipulation of political authorities. This makes for a certain resistance built into the political socialization process. A lesson quickly learned by political engineers, political educators, and political propagandists is the rigidity of the informal network of political socialization. Political elites can manipulate only at the edges of these processes. Textbooks can be changed or rewritten, political propaganda in the mass media can be altered; but the core of political socialization appears to lie in those agencies which cannot be reprogrammed quickly and effectively. The specter of *1984* notwithstanding, neither 20th-century totalitarian regimes, nor political leaders in new nations, nor democratic devotees promoting political participation, have found it easy to alter political views radically. What parent passes on to child, teacher to student, or friend to friend concerning the political world, remains unprogrammed. The experiences people have with politics in some instances may be even less manipulable. To convince a population that the political order is efficient, some efficiency must be demonstrated. Political propaganda cannot replace the tangible experiences which citizens have.

Here we note again the generally conservative bias of political socialization. To the degree that changes in political values are dependent on the political socialization processes, we expect alteration to be incremental rather than galloping. Changes will also tend to be uneven rather than consistent and systematic.

We have frequently stressed the theme that political socialization processes are essentially conservative forces in society. Before leaving this observation, we should append one major qualification. It is not in error to say that political socialization is a conserving force, but neither is it to say so completely accurate. The more accurate statement is one which suggests that political socialization is a molding force. Man is fairly plastic. The very notion of social self, from which is drawn the idea of political self, implies this. It is true that in the overwhelming number of cases social institutions are geared to

producing citizens who more or less replicate their predeces-
sors. In this sense political socialization is conservative. But
there is nothing inherent in the process to make it so. The
powerful molding possibilities in political socialization can be
adapted to radical and total alterations as well — if not as
easily as they have been adapted to incremental changes and
protection of the social order.

Cases of individual transformation are well known. Psychi-
atric case histories and religious literature testify to the possibility of total conversion. Though it is more difficult to find
examples of cultures rather than individuals undergoing total
change, such examples are available. It is important that their
rarity not obscure their theoretical importance. We can briefly
cite two relevant cases.

The history of the American Negro is a case of total and
radical cultural transformation. In a matter of a generation or
two, the Negro, brought to work the cotton plantations, ceased
to resemble his more fortunate African brethren who avoided
the slave market. The experience of being enslaved all but
annihilated the slave's cultural past. The enslavement process
was a series of severe shocks: capture in native wars or raiding
parties, the long march to the seaport, sale to slave traders, the
dread middle passage, the humiliation of the market in the
West Indies, and the chattel status which meant total denial
of any human rights.

Only one out of three West Africans survived this hor-
rendous journey. The survivors quickly discovered that the
old values no longer had any meaning. A completely new life,
separated from the previous life by a series of terrible experiences, meant that the old ways had to be discarded. We suspect that the first generation slave did not really "forget" his
name, his family, his religion, his homeland, his language. But
he found them irrelevant to his new status. Survival depended
on the slave master, and he was not often tolerant of the
"primitive" cultural forms of the slave's native West Africa. It
is small wonder that native culture was discarded and that
the American Negro bears so little resemblance to his African
forebears.

Another, more recent example of extreme cultural transformation occurred in the Nazi concentration camps. Studies of the effects of German concentration camp experiences present a bleak picture. Inmates who survived the arrest in the middle of the night, cattle-car transportation, initial platform "selection," indignities of the SS guards, frequent physical pain, constant psychological tensions, loss of the past, and bewilderment about the future, underwent profound personality changes. The concentration camp inmate bore little resemblance to the free man he once had been. Nor is the man who returned to "normal" life after the concentration camp simply an extension of his childhood years. The intervening experience was too awful to forget.

The lessons of American slavery and German concentration camps are an important corrective to any tendency to impute conservatism as a necessary component of political socialization. Under conditions of severe dislocation, man can undergo extensive personality and cultural alteration. Circumstances can bring about massive changes in political views. The fact that the informality and diffuseness of the political socialization process make it difficult to transform cultural patterns does not mean such transformation is impossible.

SOME LITTLE UNDERSTOOD ASPECTS

We have offered some summary thoughts about what is generally known about political socialization. We turn now to an outline of things we do not know about this process, to the gaps in our summary statement. Again the goal is to be selective rather than exhaustive. Four topics will point out the gaps in our knowledge: (1) questions about cultural variations; (2) questions about the interaction among the various political socialization agencies; (3) questions about how collective experiences of the social system are translated through the political socialization mechanisms; and (4) questions about social and political change.

1. *Cultural Variations.* The thoughts argued in this chapter impose homogeneity and order upon processes which are really heterogeneous and complex. We have discussed political socialization in this volume as if we were referring to a universal phenomenon, while basing our discussion upon findings drawn

for the most part from American and Western societies. Our
goal (a discussion of political socialization as a universal phenomenon), coupled with lack of data from non-Western societies, has made this problem inevitable.

Rates of learning, variations in the influence of different
agents of political socialization, relationships among the agents
of political socialization, connections between formal and informal learning experiences, the degree of congruence between
early and late socialization, all are likely to vary from culture
to culture. A systematically comparative scheme is necessary. It
would show how political systems (or types of systems) differ
in the performance of political socialization. In the text we
have offered where we could some hypotheses about cultural
differences we have found. More often than not these differences are evident between traditional, transitional, and modern polities.

Differences are not all at the national level; there are also
considerable variations among cultural groups within the same
nation. Patterns of political learning are not alike for all population groupings. Some groups experience political socialization in forms quite different from others. It is not possible to
list, or even to suggest, all these subgroup variations. The
reader should be aware that examples or statements pertaining
to any given nation often overlook considerable variation
among population subgroupings. Class differences, for instance,
are significant for socialization in many countries. A comparison of the political learning experiences of upper class children
with lower class children often shows as many differences as a
comparison between two nations.

There is little point in saying more about this major qualification. We have pointed out these limitations in the course of
the discussion. A comprehensive theory of political socialization must be sensitive to such variations. To say that there
are important intercultural differences in political socialization
does not mean that there are not at the same time universal
aspects to the process. Our discussion in this chapter is based
on the proposition that there are universally applicable aspects
of political learning. It is not possible now to identify the

universals and separate them from the culturally determined factors.

2. *Interaction Among Political Socialization Agencies.* Our lack of information about the different influences of various agencies is considerable. We have attempted to suggest some relationships in this chapter and in previous sections of the book. Much still remains in doubt. These are a few of the more obvious questions: How cumulative is political socialization? What happens when two political socialization agencies, with different messages, compete for the individual? Can later socialization experiences attenuate the values acquired during childhood, and if so under what conditions? How basic are the early acquired "basic orientations"?

The argument presented here is somewhat misleading with regard to these questions. The development of profile implies that all political socialization agencies operate in roughly the same direction and with the same general intent. But as the findings we have presented suggest, they do not always do so. In fact, they may rarely do so. Except in the most stable and coherent of societies, people must "unlearn" as well as learn. We have pointed out that political socialization processes can never fully anticipate the future. There will always be some discontinuity between agencies operating during different periods in the individual's life. Those questions left unanswered by our overly simplistic presentation here are of considerable theoretical and research interest.

3. *Social Events and Political Socialization.* Our summary framework may be misleading in yet another way. It stresses the way in which *individuals* move through the political socialization process. Yet we know that entire societies experience political events in ways that leave a lasting mark on their political culture. Wars, depressions, and revolutions are the most extreme examples of such events.

An individually biased summary does not inform us about these "societal" events. It does not tell us how the collective experiences of a nation become part of the political culture, how they are transmitted from generation to generation. Wars, depressions, population movements, invasions, revolutions, and so forth, happen to whole populations. The developmental profile of any individual will be affected substantially if he lives through a period of cataclysmic social change and cultural transformation.

A comprehensive theory of political socialization must isolate the mechanisms which transmit these collective events. We suspect that the agencies we have talked about do so, but do not know precisely how they do it. In other words, it is important that the reader not take our summary for more than it is. The summary does not help us with some of the larger, harder-to-deal-with questions of political socialization. One of these questions is how collective experiences become part of the political memory and the political socialization processes of a nation.

4. *Processes of Change.* Finally, and following directly from the preceding point, much of what we have said leaves us in doubt about certain processes of change. We have depicted an essentially conservative process, despite our constant referral to issues of change and instability. The process is conservative because parents (and other socialization agencies) tend to teach their children the things they themselves learned as children. However, we do know that major changes in political cultures take place. One factor accounting for such changes is the intrusion of cataclysmic events. But changes of considerable magnitude take place in less dramatic ways as well.

One such change is the issue of cultural evolution, perhaps one of the oldest and least understood concepts in social science. Students of society have long sought adequate explanations of social change, but no satisfactory, comprehensive theory has been developed. In the mid-twentieth century, we are still searching for an explanation of the mechanisms which transform one network of social relations, one pattern of cultural values, into another. Scholars have yet to identify with any precision the units which make for change, which shuffle and regroup the cultural patterns whose mutations are the raw material for new cultural forms. As yet we can present only partial and fragmentary ideas, but political socialization theory points us toward the mechanisms of social evolution.

Index